THE THEORY AND
PRACTICE OF HYPNOTISM

In non-technical language this book gives practical
instruction in hypnotic techniques.

D1150512

THE THEORY AND PRACTICE OF HYPNOTISM

by

William J. Ousby

THORSONS PUBLISHERS LIMITED
Wellingborough, Northamptonshire

First published 1967
Seventh Impression 1982
First published in this format 1984
Second Impression 1986

British Library Cataloguing in Publication Data

Ousby, William J.
    The theory and practice of hypnotism.
    1. Hypnotism
    I. Title
    154.7   BF1141

    ISBN 0-7225-0944-8

Printed in Great Britain by
Richard Clay (The Chaucer Press) Ltd,
Bungay, Suffolk

CONTENTS

INTRODUCTION

This is not a book about hypnosis, but is a practical Course of instruction which for some years was privately circulated. It has been revised and is now available in its present form.

The language throughout is non-technical and, in addition to comprehensive instructions, the book contains a summary of the fields in which hypnosis could have value.

Foremost amongst these would be the benefits which hypnosis could bring about through incorporation in the National Health Service, but, in putting forward this suggestion I am well aware of the critical shortage of doctors available to deal with the ever increasing number of sufferers from psychosomatic illness. This shortage would, in some measure, be alleviated by an Auxiliary Medical Register of responsible hypnotherapists. Working under the supervision of doctors they could conduct Hypnotherapy Clinics, to which overworked doctors could send tense and worried patients to be taught how to relax their minds and bodies. This recommendation of an expanded Preventive Health Service, using hypnotherapy in group treatment, is dealt with in Chapter Fifteen.

In persenting this book, and a plea for incorporation of hypnosis in the National Health Service, it is with the hope that it may make some small contribution to shortening the time before hypnosis is used more widely, and many years of illness and suffering on the part of tens of thousands of people, prevented.

10 Harley Street W.1

CHAPTER ONE

USES OF HYPNOSIS

This is not a treatise on the history of hypnotism, but a practical manual of hypnotic techniques. It is not necessary to have any particular type of personality to be a hypnotist. Any man or woman of average intelligence can learn to hypnotise others, but indefinable elements in one man's personality will enable him to become successful as an hypnotist, just as one man will become a more skilful musician than another. The old idea of an hypnotist, as a dominant personality with piercing eyes is quite fallacious. On the contrary an unobtrusive manner, and a quiet monotonous voice, is a very definite advantage when carrying out certain methods of hypnotic induction.

All the methods in this book are concerned with Hetero-hypnosis (hypnotising other people), with the exception of Chapters 13 and 14, which are devoted to Self Hypnosis.

The main difference between a hypnotist and the average individual is that the hypnotist possesses, and has the skill to employ the techniques which are contained in the following pages. Until comparatively recently practitioners of hypnotism, that is doctors and lay practitioners, were unwilling to disclose their methods, with the result that the subject is still surrounded by misconceptions.

The methods which hypnotists employ can be explained and, if carefully carried out, it is a frequent occurrence for a successful hypnotic induction to be effected by the student hypnotist at his first attempt.

At one time people believed that a hypnotist possessed some special secret. Actually there is no one secret, but there are a number of simple instructions which must be observed. If these are carried out with someone who is willing to co-operate, the hypnotic state is quite likely to follow as a natural consequence. The difference is that some people may take much longer to hypnotise than others. There are many different ways of inducing a hypnotic trance a number of which are explained later in this course.

The following instructions explain various tests employed in choosing subjects to hypnotise, how to overcome resistances to trance induction, and in short, a summary of the techniques of the professional hypnotist. It is not generally realised that there are many ways in which practical use can be made of the hypnotic techniques. Before proceeding with the instructions, a brief résumé of some of the fields in which hypnotism is employed now follows.

Therapeutic Uses

Hypnotism is now proving to be of very great value in therapeutic work. Seldom a week passes without some fresh report of successful cures being achieved by the use of hypnotic treatment. It is apparent that to engage in any therapeutic work, presupposes at least some knowledge of the elements of psychology and medicine. This is because some of the psychosomatic symptoms of a nervous individual so closely resemble the early symptoms of a more serious illness that ability to recognise suspicious symptoms is necessary.

However, in practice, the lay hypnotist will seldom meet a patient who has not already exhausted the possibilities of successful treatment on orthodox lines. If a patient is relying on the hypnotherapist for guidance, where there is any suspicion of anything of a serious nature, an examination should be made by a doctor, and the fact established that the difficulties complained of do not arise from a physical cause or, alternatively, do not respond to orthodox treatment.

Hypnotic suggestion is used in conjunction with many forms of therapeutic treatment, and, in many cases, enables a hypnotherapist to treat cases successfully when all other methods of treatment have failed. Whilst it is easy to become enthusiastic when it is realised that hypnotism has effected cures of many ailments and also that it is the only anaesthetic which has had no fatalities, it must be realised that it must not be used indiscriminately as a pain killer. It must not be forgotten that pain and worry are nature's signals indicating some problem or physical condition which may require attention. No treatment should be given without medical guidance or supervision.

Hypnoanalysis

Hypnoanalysis is the name that is given to a method of conducting what is virtually a telescoped psychoanalysis. Psychoanalysis, as many readers will be aware, came into being largely as the result of hypnotic experiments, and was used for some time as a means of discovering something of the hidden form, content and operations of the unconscious mind.

Since the beginning of the century psychoanalysis has established a sound empirical groundwork, and with other branches of medical science is making increasing use of hypnotism as a tool. The undue expectations of the early analysts in the curative powers of hypnotism were seen to have arisen out of a confusion between the means and the end. Hypnotism by itself was a tool—a means to an end—and needed insight. This has been in large measure achieved in the last fifty years. That is to say by the knowledge, skill and insight of the hypnotherapist. The power of hypnotism to correct faulty behaviour and assist in adaptation is determined by how far the inner resistances and injuries are perceived and effective measures devised for dealing with them.

As an Aid to Family, Friends and Children

There are many cases where a knowledge of hypnotism enables friends or relatives to give aid or treatment to each other. If they learn how to administer hypnotic suggestions to each other, husbands and wives, friends and relatives can mutually assist each other to sleep more soundly, to achieve increased confidence, to relax, to break bad habits, and to stop worrying. They can also help to remedy or relieve many disabilities and illnesses, particularly where there is the need to repeat suggestions regularly for a period, and the aid of a professional hypnotist is not available. Parents in particular can do much to aid their children in helping them to sleep soundly, in ridding them of nervousness and bad habits, freeing them from "examination nerves," improving concentration and memory, and thus helping them with their school work and education, and generally building up morale, but it is advised that no practical experiments are carried out until the course has been thoroughly studied.

As an Aid to Business and Professional People

A knowledge of hypnotism enables the doctor, osteopath, dental surgeon, masseur, lay practitioner, solicitor and teacher to speak with greater authority and assurance. This does not mean that they will openly employ hypnotism. One of the most important of the techniques of hypnotism is "waking suggestion," which is positively employed suggestion without any "formal" induction. "Masked" waking suggestions can be administered through the medium of general conversation, or during an interview. Many business executives, doctors, teachers and officials who deal with the public are already unconsciously using hypnotic techniques in primitive form. If they understand hypnotism they will act with greater certainty and confidence. There is little doubt that most of the outstanding leaders in politics, industry, and in many other fields have consciously or unconsciously a sound working knowledge of hypnotic techniques, and this, in large measure, is the explanation of their ability to influence and control others.

Hypnotic suggestion is frequently the means of helping people to increase the quantity and quality of their work. Artists and writers whose creative ability seems to have temporarily dried up find in hypnotic suggestion a means of re-creating inspirational moods. Politicians, actors and public speakers who have become tense, and wish to relax or to increase their confidence, also benefit from the use of hypnotic suggestion.

Self Hypnosis

It has been maintained that all hypnosis is basically self hypnosis, that is to say it is the subject's uncritical acceptance of the hynotist's suggestions which, in a large measure, bring about the trance state. There is much to support this view. The hypnotic subject does not, of course, realise that it is his unquestioning acceptance of suggestion which enables the trance state to be induced, for successful suggestion is seldom recognised as such. Suggestion subtly influences people without their knowledge.

Self suggestion often manifests itself to people in everyday life in the form of spontaneous thoughts or observations. Often it would be difficult to decide whether some thoughts could be classed as justifiable observations, or as negative self suggestions. Thoughts such as "I'll never be able to do this", or "I cannot stop smoking, however hard I try" are often potent negative self suggestions, keeping alive habits which would weaken and fade if positive suggestions were substituted.

If an individual is unaware that he is using negative suggestion he may be causing himself all manner of disabilities or ailments. Fortunately suggestion is a two edged sword, and, as self hypnosis is a concentrated form of self suggestion, those who are instructed in its use can proceed to cure the ills and ailments which negative suggestion may have caused.

Successful self suggestion succeeds because it short circuits the judgment and, in this way, gains access to the unconscious mind. The knowledge and skill to do this form an important part of the hypnotist's technique, and for this reason self hypnosis is dealt with in later chapters.

In Psychological and Psychical Research

The changes in the state of consciousness brought about through hypnotic suggestions can lead to the development of faculties which would otherwise remain dormant. Some of the remarkable experiments which are possible under hypnotic control would be of very great interest to students of psychology, and psychical research. These include:

Hyperacuity

Hyperacuity is a condition which may be produced by suggestion in many hypnotic subjects. It is a hypersensitivity of the senses. By suggesting to a hypnotic subject that any of his senses will become more acute it is possible that the efficiency of that sense may temporarily be increased, for example, a good hypnotic subject may be made to hear minute sounds or to detect things which he would not normally see or hear in waking consciousness, and which would be inaudible or not be perceived by a normal person. This hyperacuity can increase the senses of hearing, touch, smell, taste and also of vision. In the latter case the subject will have to be in a deep somnambulistic trance so that his eyes may be opened without breaking the trance. Individuals vary greatly in their responses. In some cases suggestions to render a sense more acute will have no effect, and with others the most surprising results will be obtained. Normally hyperacuity is present only when the individual is actually hypnotised, but sometimes this hypersensitivity will persist for a period after the trance as a result of post-hypnotic suggestions directing that this ability will be retained on waking.

Regression

Through hypnotic suggestion the subject is able to move backwards in time, and recover memories which normally he would be unable to recall by an act of will. By this method very early memories can be recovered. Regression in this way has very great value in the diagnostic field. This facility also applies to the recalling of dreams which would not be remembered but for the power of hypnotic suggestion to regress the hypnotised subject.

This is not a complete summary of all the fields in which hynotism can be employed. Amongst those uses not mentioned are the teaching or aiding of others to acquire proficiency in a wide variety of subjects such as learning shorthand, typing, to play musical instruments, swimming, dancing, and as an auxiliary in many professions. Instructions for the first practical steps in becoming a hypnotist are given in the following sections.

The unconscious processes governing the emotional and physical life have their roots deep in, and are nourished from the source of life itself. Contact with this deeper source of life can be achieved by means of the hypnotic and self hypnotic techniques, when allied with a sincere attempt on the part of the individual to carry out his true role in the broader scheme of life.

CHAPTER TWO

CHEVREUL'S PENDULUM

There are various tests which are used to select the people most susceptible to hypnotic suggestion. These tests are by no means infallible. Frequently those who have not responded well to the initial tests may prove later to be excellent hypnotic subjects. Carrying out these tests gives the student hypnotist an excellent opportunity of practising the technique of making suggestions.

A classic test of self suggestion which the reader can experiment with for himself was named after Chevreul, a distinguished chemist and Director of the Natural History Museum in Paris. He was reputed to be the only man of world wide fame whose centenary was celebrated in his own lifetime. He lived to the age of 103. He investigated the apparently inexplicable movements of the pendulum used by mediums and clairvoyants.

An Example of Unconscious Self Suggestion

Usually the pendulum was a ring suspended by a thread and held near a wine glass. The ring would swing, apparently of its own accord, and tap out messages on the wine glass, one for A, two for B or some such code. Chevreul proved by a series of experiments that though people could be acting in perfectly good faith, the movements of the pendulum were caused by almost imperceptible muscular movements of the hand holding the thread; in other words the pendulum's movements were caused by involuntary movements on the part of the individual holding the ring who was completely unaware of the unconscious movements of his hand.

In these cases the movements were caused by unconscious suggestion, and it is now recommended that the reader himself carries out the experiment on the following lines.

A Suggestion Experiment on Yourself

Take a small weight, to which a thread can be attached—a ring, or small key, will serve admirably. When you have tied the weight to the end of the thread, tie the other end of the thread to the end of a pencil so that it forms, as it were, a miniature fishing rod and line, the pencil being the rod, and the thread (which should be about eight inches long) forming the fishing line, with the weight suspended at the end of it. This device is known as Chevreul's Pendulum. Take a sheet of paper and on it draw a straight, bold line about six inches long. After placing the paper on the table or the floor, hold the miniature fishing line with finger and thumb at the other end to which the thread is tied, so that the weight is suspended over the line you have drawn, about one inch from the paper. Direct your gaze intently on the line, and in a short space of time the weight will, apparently *of its own accord*, begin to sway backwards and forwards following the direction of the line. It is almost uncanny, once the pendulum has got on the move, to watch its performance—it will increase the arc of its swing backwards and forwards quite briskly. Whilst it is in motion move the paper round so that the line now points in a different direction— keep your eyes steadily on the line and, in a few minutes, the pendulum will also alter its direction and will again swing along the line.

Second Stage in Experiment

When the pendulum has responded well, draw a second line at right angles to the first, hold the pendulum over these lines, at the intersection of the two, and it will be found that it will invariably travel up and down the line *on which you direct your attention*. After this has been successfully accomplished, draw a circle. It will be found that the pendulum will swing in a circle *when you direct your attention on the circle*.

If, at the first attempt the pendulum does not respond immediately, do not be discouraged. With the majority of people some movement begins within the first minute, whilst with others a number of sittings may be necessary before the facility is acquired. In cases where the pendulum does not respond this is due, either to inattention, mind wandering, or unconscious sabotage. In all cases progress will be made with patience and practice.

Some readers might feel inclined to resent the accusation of inattention or unconscious sabotage, but when we examine the mechanics underlying the behaviour of Chevreul's Pendulum, it will be appreciated that OUR UNCONSCIOUS ATTITUDE towards the experiment is the dominant factor. The movement of the pendulum is actually caused by imperceptible movements of our hands, though WE ARE QUITE UNAWARE OF THE FACT. The conscious mind is keenly intent on what is happening in the role of an observer, and until his attention is drawn to the fact is unaware of the compulsive influence which suggestion is exercising.

A Suggestion Experiment on Somebody Else

This experiment is to be carried out not only on oneself, but on others. Ask someone else to hold the pencil and instruct him to direct his gaze on the line which has been drawn on the paper. The suggestion is then put to him that the pendulum will sway along the line and, in the majority of cases it will do so. If the subject says or thinks: "It is not moving," or "I don't think it will work with me," then it will not move. This is because he has unconsciously or consciously accepted the suggestion that it will not move and the negative suggestion has become effective.

Get the subject to hold the pencil whilst standing up. See he keeps his elbow away from his side, and stands back about eighteen inches from the table. Concentrate first on one line and, when the pendulum has obeyed this suggestion, then on the other. Suggest: "It will now swing in a small circle—now the circle will grow." Then say to him: "In a few moments it is going to stop," then wait. It may take a little while, but gradually the pendulum will come to rest and hang down perfectly still. If he thinks it will move in a straight line in any desired direction, it will do so, if he thinks it will move in a large circle, a small circle, an ellipse, or that it will stand still, it will obey his instructions. The proficiency of the individual in this experiment will increase as his nerves and muscles become educated in making the imperceptible movements which cause the pendulum to move, though he is himself not consciously aware he is causing the movements

The purpose in carrying out this experiment is to demonstrate that if an idea is accepted by the unconscious mind, it automatically becomes true, also for the reader to begin practising making suggestions to other people.

CHAPTER THREE

SUGGESTIBILITY TESTS

The next step is to find someone who is willing to co-operate in further experiments. Explain to your fellow experimentor the object is to demonstrate that the more we know about suggestion, the more we are able to employ it for the benefit of others as well as ourselves.

For your own part, regard the exercises as purely experimental. Be prepared for failure or only partial success, but do not let this deter you, as the object of these preliminary experiments is to gain practical experience.

The following experiment can be tried on someone else without the necessity of an explanation. It offers an excellent illustration of the difference between theoretical and practical knowledge on the most important subject of relaxation.

Relaxation Test

To carry out this experiment, ask a friend to stand up and look straight ahead. Ask him to raise one of his arms to shoulder level. Place one of your hands under his upper arm, and the other under his hand whilst standing in front of him. His arm will now be supported in a horizontal position by your two hands. Tell him to relax the muscles of his arm, repeating the instruction several times. Then ask him if he has done so. Keep your own hands perfectly steady during this procedure. When, in response to your enquiry, he tells you his arm is relaxed, withdraw your hands suddenly. If his arm muscles have been completely relaxed, his arm will immediately drop limply to his side. If there has been only a partial relaxation, the arm will fall slowly. If there has been no relaxation the arm will remain outstretched. If your subject has failed to relax correctly, explain to him that though we may believe we know what relaxation is, in actual fact we may fail in a practical sense to achieve it. Repeat the experiment until your subject grasps the idea; you can vary the procedure by using the other arm, then both arms together, bringing both arms out in front instead of sideways.

Swaying Test

For your next test, explain first to your subject that you are now going to demonstrate how suggestion affects the imagination. Ask him to stand erect with his feet close together. Tell him to close his eyes, make his mind a blank and listen to you. Now tell him that he will be unable to stand perfectly still because he will start to sway slightly from side to side. Tell him that the harder he tries to maintain his balance, the more difficult it will become. Watch his movements and amplify your suggestions with appropriate comments such as: "Now you are swaying to the right ... and now to the left. ... Now you are swaying backwards ... and now forwards ..." etc. Keep up these suggestions for a minute or two. There is a close parallel to be drawn between this experiment, and the exercise of Chevreul's Pendulum. The muscular movements are in both cases due to suggestion.

Do not feel disappointed if your subject remained immovable. The reason for the failure may have been because the subject selected was consciously or unconsciously not co-operating, or perhaps because your suggestions were unconvincing, or some outside disturbance may have distracted his attention. There are many reasons why suggestions, both to ourselves and others, may fail from time to time. Do not be disappointed but analyse what has happened, remember the main object of your experiment at this stage is to gain experience.

Swaying Test—Second Stage

Next, ask your subject to stand upright again with his eyes closed and feet together. Stand behind him and say: "I am going to place my fingers on the back of your neck ... there!" at the same time firmly pressing your fingers on the base of his skull. Then say: "I am going to draw my finger backwards gently, and you will find yourself swaying backwards with it." Assure him that he will not fall because you will stop him as soon as he begins to sway backwards. Then very steadily and slowly draw your hand backwards, and he will, if your suggestion has been convincing, start to sway backwards. Stop him by placing your hand on his shoulder. Repeat this experiment several times.

It is better to keep your subject's attention engaged so, even if what you say is somewhat repetitive, continue to comment authoritatively on the way suggestion, playing on the imagination, influences our actions. These "explanations" play an important part in the experiments, for they provide the opportunity of planting suggestions in the subject's mind. If the average subject implicitly accepts your word that what you suggest will happen in an experiment, then, almost invariably, it will happen. If, on the other hand, he is critical or antagonistic the experiment will, in all probability, be a failure or only partially successful. Therefore, in making your suggestions, phrase what you say in such a manner as to be acceptable to the subject and not likely to arouse any unconscious resentment.

Swaying Test—Third Stage

Proceed to say something on the following lines: "The success of this experiment depends entirely on your ability to keep your mind clear—just push all other thoughts out of your mind and listen to me. I am going to place my finger tips on your temples—so—and as I draw my hands forward you will find yourself swaying forward." Whilst giving these instructions illustrate what you are saying by placing your fingers on *your own* temples, and as you say the above words—"you will find yourself swaying forward" illustrate by actually swaying forward yourself. This little illustration, if deftly executed, exercises considerable influence on the subject. Next say: "That's right, put your feet closer together. Your toes as well as your heels; stand to attention, hold your head up and look straight at me, *just balancing upright.*" Note the emphasised words; these are significant. As you say them put your hands on the subject's shoulders, and gently sway him backwards an inch or so, then bring him forward again to the upright. See that he does not move his feet, and that he does not raise himself up on his toes. Now rock him gently backwards and forwards several times telling him to let himself balance upright. The object of this is to loosen his calf muscles and see that they are not rigidly braced. When ready tell your subject to look straight at you, to keep his mind clear, and whilst you are talking, stretch out your arms towards him and place your fingers lightly on his temples. Continue talking, and at what you judge to be the right moment, or if you feel a slight forward movement, draw your hands towards you, keeping your fingers still on his temples. At the same time say: "You are coming forward, forward, forward." A slow movement and considerable practice is necessary to calculate just when, and at what rate, the hands are to be moved. You can vary this experiment if you wish by having the subject close his eyes, and keeping them closed throughout the test.

Locking Subject's Hands

For the next attempt instruct your subject to clasp his hands together. The standing position is best, but he may be seated if you wish. The palms of his hands should be pushed hard against each other, and his fingers interlaced. Now ask him to think that his hands are so tightly fastened together that he will be unable to move them. Tell him to think that his hands have become stuck together, and to keep repeating it to himself. Instruct him to look straight at you and, under no circumstances, to look away. Now place your hands outside his and press his hands together, at the same time looking at him steadily and saying: "Press them together firmer, tighter, tighter still; they are beginning to stick, they are sticking together tightly, you will not be able to get them apart; the harder you try the more impossible it will be." Then pause and pronounce firmly, "Your hands are tightly fastened together—you cannot unclasp them...." Remove your own hands from his but continue to gaze fixedly at him and continue your suggestions. Some people however hard they try will be unable to get their hands apart. If he is unable to unclasp his hands, say to him in a quiet and confident manner, "All right, stop trying, I am going to count and when I get to 'Three' you will be able to unclasp them ... One, Two, Three, open them." He will then be able to open them for your earlier suggestions have been neutralised. It is much easier to remove this effect than produce it. The influence of your suggestions is likely to weaken as soon as your suggestions cease, or your subject looks away.

Armchair Test

Another conditioning test, is to tell the subject to sit in an armchair with his legs stretched out and his arms relaxed. When he is comfortably relaxed tell him he is not to move his arms or legs, and that when his eyes are closed he will find that he is unable to stand up. Then tell him impressively to close his eyes. If all these instructions are given in an authoritative manner the subject, in all probability will not be able to stand up. The loss of volitional control experienced by the subject will be commensurate with the measure with which he has accepted the instruction affecting the movement of his limbs. It is manifestly impossible to get out of the chair without establishing a new centre of gravity which would involve the movements of the limbs.

The success of these experiments depends on your ability to give the instructions with such conviction that they are accepted and believed by the subject without question.

Analysing Your Experiments

Regard these tests as experiments in suggestion which is what they are. If your experiments were only partly effective, think about what has occurred. Discuss his experience with your subject. Try and discover the causes of failure. Often they are obvious; some noises or distraction, unsteadiness in your voice, some hesitation in your manner. Sometimes it may be simply the fact that your subject did not understand your meaning, due to some slight ambiguity in speech. Discuss the matter thoroughly; find out what he thinks about the experiments—what his reactions are. Reverse the roles and get him to make the same suggestions to you. This will give you some idea of how you react to suggestion.

CHAPTER FOUR

PRE-CONDITIONS FOR HYPNOTISING

To explain how to hypnotise an individual is not difficult. To put that advice into practice is an entirely
different matter. It is, in a sense, a creative work; for
example, anyone can get paints, brushes and canvas,
but it requires an artist to paint a picture. The hypnotist's canvas is the subject's mind. He paints with words
and actions. If he uses them aright he has a hypnotised
subject, and if he doesn't he fails. In the main, ninety
per cent of the work is done beforehand by the hypnotist on himself, so that he may be able to adapt himself
to the various situations which arise.

What Prospective Subjects Think

Consideration must be given to what is happening in
the subject's mind before the attempt to hypnotise him
is made. If your proposed subject is in any way uneasy,
or expresses any unwillingness, it is wisest to find another subject. It is extremely unlikely that you would
get any results, and there is always the possibility that
an awkward or invidious situation would arise. Never
lose sight of the fact that there still exists a fair amount
of prejudice against hypnotism.

Subjects' Misconceptions About Hypnosis

Among the people who wish to be hypnotised will be
some whose attitude towards hynotism will be found to
be a mixture of fear and superstition. These are people
who have either seen a crude stage presentation, or who

have drawn their ideas from old wives' tales or sensational novels. Don't argue with them, merely assure them that it is a very pleasant experience which, in all probability, will help them. If they have read articles in magazines or newspapers of the successful treatment of many complaints by hypnotism, their attitude, generally speaking, will be a rational approach. If you are talking to a reasonable individual, who has some slight knowledge of the subject, put his mind at rest so that you can be assured of his intelligent co-operation. In the main, take him into your confidence as fully as possible. If later he finds that you have misled him, or have not fully explained matters, his confidence in you may be destroyed. If what you have promised, or said, is found to be correct, his faith in you is strengthened.

Before attempting any experiments, careful attention must be given to the attitude of the prospective subject. Has he any interest in hypnotism? How will it benefit him to be hypnotised? Does he think he can be harmed or made to look foolish or do anything against his will? Is he nervous about talking and divulging secrets? He should be reassured on these points.

Be Cautious Whom You Hypnotise

Serious loss of prestige and possible complications can arise through thoughtless experimentation. The amateur hypnotist may be called upon to show his powers. He would be wise to avoid impromptu performances, nor should he engage in any experiment with a subject on whom someone is already carrying out hypnotic work. This latter circumstance may lead to considerable confusion in the subject's mind. *Under no circumstances should any reader carry out any experiments on anyone until the entire Course has been studied.*

People You MUST NOT Hypnotise

Never, under any circumstances, attempt to hypnotise anyone suffering from epilepsy or any irresponsible individual or anyone who shows any symptoms of being hysterical, nor should you attempt to hypnotise a woman with any neurotic or hysterical symptoms except in the presence of some reliable witnesses. The complications that can arise here will be readily grasped when it is realised that the recollections of the individual who has been hypnotised can be very vague and hazy, but this does not in any way interfere with what they may imagine. Thus, a hysterical patient whose trance recollections are confused with wish fulfilment, can quite easily cause a most invidious situation for the hypnotist. There is no doubt the hypnotist needs more protection from the public than the public from the hypnotist. There are also possibilities of complications arising where hypnotic suggestions of any inhibitions of physical movement or function may provide a hysterical patient with a ready-made mechanism for escaping from reality. This is something which should be borne in mind. Unless the reader has considerable psychological knowledge it is better to avoid hysterical subjects.

People Most Easily Hypnotised

Men and women seem to be equally good as hypnotic subjects. Generally speaking those who follow some organised calling, such as the police, the army or the navy, tend to be good subjects. This is because they have already acquired the ability to form reflexes and to obey orders.

Those who are most easily hypnotised are children and adolescents. Bernheim found that four children out of five could be hypnotised. From my own experience I would say the percentage is considerably higher. Younger people are more likely to obey instructions, for the commands of the parent and the teacher may have been long obeyed without question. This is precisely what is needed—obedience without any interference from the critical conscious mind. It is for this reason that the introvert character tends to be a difficult subject. He is over critical, tends to be suspicious and analyses every move. It should be remembered that in the Hypnotism Act 1952, there is a prohibition on hypnotising in public persons under the age of 21. Details of how to obtain this Act are given later.

Conditions Favourable For Inducing Hypnosis

In theory, 95 per cent of people can be hypnotised, but failure to achieve this percentage in practice arises for many reasons, including limitation of time to carry out sufficient conditioning, failure to diagnose the hidden resistances, and obscure psychological disturbances. Some of the conditions which are helpful for hypnotising are:

Fixation of attention.
Monotonous intonation of the voice.
Limitation of voluntary physical movements.
Limitation of field of voluntary consciousness.
Inhibition of all thoughts and ideas except those upon which the attention is directed.
Quietness and warm room temperature without draughts.

Pay attention to the general environment. See that the chair or couch is comfortable. See that no bright light shines directly in the eyes of your subject—if there is a strong light it is better that it shines in your face and the subject remains in the shade. The exception to this is where a bright light is actually used as a means of inducing hypnosis. Some hypnotists prefer to work in a darkened room or with a dim coloured light. An electric light bulb of 15 watt strength which fits the standard electric fitting is admirably suited for this purpose.

Your Voice and What To Say

The manner in which one speaks is all important. Use a quiet but authoritative tone of voice, which leaves no doubt that you are fully confident and know what you are doing. Whilst you are making suggestions there must be no uneasy pauses. What you are saying should flow smoothly and easily. It is wiser to memorise the phrases you are going to use so that you may speak easily and fluently when attempting an induction.

See that your subject is seated comfortably and that his clothes are not restricting his movements or that his shoes are not tight. Talk to him whilst giving him a fair amount of time to settle down. Whilst giving him instructions, you should be gaining his confidence. Don't rush things, and avoid uneasy pauses.

The Personality and Idiosyncrasies of Subject

There are now given a number of different ways of inducing a hypnotic trance. There is no one particular way which is best. One individual will adopt a method which appeals to him or suits his personality. Someone else would prefer to evolve his own particular method. The purpose for which the trance is being induced is an important factor. The personality of the subject has to be considered, and also the prestige of the hypnotist. An amateur hypnotist has a wider scope than a therapist. He can, for example, say with great emphasis:

"You cannot open your eyes." If the subject opens his eyes the hypnotist can lightly dismiss the matter and try another method, but if this happens to a therapist the loss of prestige will make further induction of the trance more difficult. Again one hypnotist will succeed in hypnotising a subject where another hypnotist has failed. The individual idiosyncrasies of the subject are also an important factor, for example, a subject with a rebellion complex will unconsciously resent a strong authoritative approach. Someone who suffers from sleeplessness is not going to respond readily to suggestions of "You are becoming sleepy." For these reasons it is necessary that the hypnotist has some knowledge of other methods. It is not suggested that the student should practise them all, but the wider his knowledge the more flexible will be his technique.

Protect Yourself Against Negative Suggestion

Be on your guard against unconscious negative suggestion when reading the following methods of hypnotising people. It is very easy to suggest to oneself that it would be impossible for something so spectacular to occur as a result of such simple actions. We can very easily miss the thing for which we are looking. When reading the following instructions, do not look for complications where they do not exist. The majority of people fail to grasp the essentials of hypnotism not because the essentials are difficult to understand, but because they are so simple that most people overlook them.

Important

Do not give any post hypnotic suggestions, or carry out any experiments until you have carefully studied the complete Course.

CHAPTER FIVE

HYPNOTISING BY FIXED GAZE

Method One

Fixation of the gaze is one method employed for hypnotising people. As the name implies, this involves gazing fixedly at an object. There are many variations of this method, some of which are given here. The reader will later probably devise variations of his own. The usual procedure is to seat the subject comfortably and take some bright object which is held in front of the subject's eyes, slightly higher than the level of the gaze and about twelve inches from his face. It is immaterial what is used as the object—a ring, the end of a silver pencil, the end of a thimble, or a light. The subject is asked to gaze steadily at the object. When the elevated position of the eyes is maintained for a short period the eye muscles will tire. This is because the eyes are pulled inwards and upwards, converging slightly, and are in an unaccustomed and strained position. This tiring, which is a physiological process, is anticipated by the hypnotist, who makes suggestions on the following lines: "Your eyes will shortly become very tired. Your eyelids will want to close," etc., etc. The subject may blink. The hypnotist will take advantage of this and comment on the fact.

The subject's eyes must be kept fixed, gazing steadily at the object. When you first notice changes in the face and the eyes, keep commenting on these changes, saying simply: "You are getting sleepier—your eyelids are getting heavier—."

To avoid needless repetition this, and the following

methods of induction, will only be described up to this light stage. Fuller and more detailed instructions for deepening the hypnotic state are given later.

Method Two

Another method of inducing hypnosis is to give the subject a small metal disc with a spot in the centre. A small piece of black cardboard with a small piece of silver paper about the size of a pea stuck in the centre will serve admirably. Place the subject comfortably sitting in a chair and get him to cup his right elbow in his left palm. In his right hand place a piece of cardboard. Have the subject direct his gaze at the piece of silver paper and tell him to concentrate his gaze upon it, and as far as possible, to exclude all thoughts. Tell him that his breathing will become deeper, and that he will notice a slight numbness in the hand that holds the card. Sit down beside him and suggest that not only will his arms become numb, but he will feel this numbness stealing over the whole of his body. Whilst you are talking watch him closely to see if his eyes, body and features are being affected by the suggestions you are making to him. When you observe any signs of this, say firmly: "Your eyes are becoming heavier and are closing," or "Your arms are becoming heavier and more tired," or: "Your breathing is becoming deeper." If his eyes do not close, give him definite instructions to close them. When they are closed instruct him to remain sitting, listening to your voice. (Continue with trance deepening method described later.)

Method Three

Another fixed gaze method which has both advantages and disadvantages is to instruct the subject to look directly at you. Tell him to look into one of your eyes.

Indicate which eye by pointing to it with your fore-finger. The reason for this is that he will find it is impossible to look into both of your eyes at the same time. Tell him that his breathing will become deeper, and he will begin to feel drowsy, and his eyes will want to close. Pause for a while and when he blinks, which he will do, tell him that his eyes are going to close when you count up to three. Tell him that they will close just after you have said the word "Three," and that then he is simply to rest and listen to your voice. His eyes may not close immediately after you have said the word "Three," in which case regard him steadily as there may be a slight pause between you having said "Three" and his eyes closing.

As a preparation to make this method of fixed gaze technique more effective, it is advisable to practise look-ing at a spot on the wall or in a mirror to strengthen your eyes against blinking.

Do not look directly into the subject's eyes, but direct your gaze in between them, at the bridge of the nose.

How To Avoid Unconsciously Hypnotising Yourself

Be on your guard against being hypnotised yourself.* This is possible when using this direct-gaze method and you are looking into the eyes of the subject. If you feel the onset of any trance, act decisively and without any hesitation. Immediately raise your hands and, with your fingers, firmly close your subject's eyelids. Whilst doing this say with firmness: "Rest, keep your eyes closed and listen to me . . ." shake off your own drowsi-ness and proceed with the trance deepening material given later.

* See *Self-Hypnosis and Scientific Self-Suggestion*, W. J. Ousby.

Method Four

An excellent method is to tell your subject to fix his gaze on some object and to follow closely your instructions. You then tell him that when you count "One," he will close his eyes, and when you count "Two," he will open them, and when you count "Three," he will close them, and on "Four," he will open them, and that he will continue to close his eyes on the odd numbers and open them on the even numbers. Inform him that as you continue to count he will find that his eyelids become heavier, that he will begin to feel drowsy. Tell him he will experience an increasing resistance to opening his eyes, which will grow so strong that in a short time he will be unable to open them, and when this occurs he is not to worry at all about it, but is to remain relaxed and continue to listen to you.

You need not give him any indication as to how long this will be, but you can, if you wish, say that by the time you have reached twenty his eyelids will have become heavy. This will be left to the reader's discretion, and his ability to judge matters of this nature will improve with experience.

Lengthening Pause After Odd Numbers

When you start to count, let the pause following the odd numbers be longer than that following the even numbers. There is no need to be diffident about this, but firmly make a longer pause after the "One," than after the "Two." The result of this is that the subject's eyes are closed for a longer period than they are open. Do not break the rhythm which you will employ in the counting as this should convey a smooth feeling of rhythm. This will prevent any tenseness and uncertainty, which are precisely the things to avoid. This method will lend itself to comments which you may make to amplify your suggestions. If the subject does not respond fairly easily, for example, you might employ something on the following lines:

"19. . . . 20 . 21. . . . You are feeling very comfortable. 22 . 23. . . . It is very pleasant just resting. 24 . 25. . . . Your eyes are getting heavier and heavier. 26 . 27. . . . It's becoming more and more of an effort, they're getting heavier and heavier, . . . becoming too much of an effort. They are getting so heavy that you will find that you cannot open them, and it is much more pleasant just to sit resting, because your eyelids have become so heavy that all you want to do is to rest." It will be noted that all comments are made on the odd numbers, whilst the subject's eyes are closed, and continue with trance deepening material given later.

Method Five

For this method use a blue electric light bulb, preferably focusing it on a small spot on the ceiling, with the rest of the room in subdued light. Make sure that the lighted spot can be seen easily by the subject, without effort. He is instructed to gaze at this blue spot of light while "sleep" suggestions on the lines dealt with later are made to him. It is interesting to note that some years ago a Government Bulletin commented on the fact that glass painters using cobalt blue sometimes fall asleep at their easels. This can be regarded as definite evidence that sleep or trance brought on by gazing at blue light is not entirely dependent on the suggestions employed.

CHAPTER SIX

ADDITIONAL HYPNOTISING TECHNIQUES

Method Six

Another method of inducing hypnosis is to seat the subject in a chair and give him the following instructions. "I want you to close your eyes. In a few moments I am going to place my finger in the centre of your forehead." After you have made general suggestions of drowsiness and heaviness of the eyes, place your forefinger gently on the centre of his forehead. Continue your instructions and suggestions on these lines: "Although your eyes are closed, I want you to direct them so that you are looking where my finger touches your forehead. Continue to look there. As you do so your breathing will get deeper." (See further instructions later.)

Method Seven

Dr. Esdaile's method was carried out in a darkened room. After the subject had been instructed to close his eyes and to relax either in a sitting or a lying position, Dr. Esdaile used to make slow passes with his hands over the body from head to feet, without touching his subject. What may be the value of the methods which make use of passes, the reader must decide for himself when he has more practical experience. There is much evidence to show that they are capable of influencing the subject. These methods were described either as "passes with contact," or "passes without contact." In the former case the hypnotist actually touches the body or limbs of the individual as he makes the pass, and in the other the passes are made without the hands actually touching the body. In these latter passes, the hands move within three or four inches of the subject's body. Early mesmerists and hypnotists used to make these passes with magnets. The results they achieved were undoubtedly due to suggestion. It is impossible to state to what extent suggestion is responsible for the result produced where the methods of mesmeric passes are used. Those who use these methods claim a deeper trance is possible by this means, but very often they lose sight of the fact that, if the same period of time were spent in inducing a trance by verbal suggestion, an equally deep trance would probably be induced. It is prudent, in speaking of a subject like hypnotism in which there are so many variable and unknown factors, to avoid dogmatism.

Whatever may be thought of Dr. Esdaile's hypnotic techniques, during the last century he performed some hundreds of surgical operations in India in which hypnotic suggestion was the only anaesthetic used.

Method Eight [*Arm Levitation Experiment*]

Having instructed your subject to sit down, without any attempt at formal induction explain that you are about to carry out a further experiment. Direct him to sit relaxed and easy in his chair and to place his hands on his knees. Tell him, by using suggestion, that you will make him feel that one arm has become lighter than the other. Spread out his fingers and let his hands rest on his knees, then say to him something on the following lines:

"I want you to look straight ahead, to go on breathing normally. Don't try to think of what I am saying, but just look at—(indicate a spot at eye level ahead of the subject)—whilst I am talking you will notice that your breathing becomes deeper. Take no notice of this, but continue to look at this spot ahead. You will also be conscious of the weight of your body. You will feel the chair where you are resting on it. You will become conscious of your clothes touching you, of your tongue in your mouth, and of your eyes feeling rather heavy. Your eyes will not close, but your breathing will become deeper. Do not think about what I am saying but simply listen to my voice. Do not think whilst I talk, but your right hand will shortly feel different from your left. There is a difference in the sensations—the left hand is feeling heavier and you have a strange feeling in your right hand. It will seem to you as though one hand is pressing down and the other is rising. In a few moments you will feel one of the fingers of your right hand will move. Do not think about it. It may be some minutes before this happens, but simply go on resting and listen to my voice. You will feel a sensation as though your right hand is going to rise up in the air, like a balloon. It will rise slowly as though it is lighter than air. You will notice that your breathing has become deeper. Push all thoughts out of your mind and simply listen to my voice." Whilst you are talking, observe your subject closely. You will probably notice a twitch or movement of one of the fingers. If this occurs, comment on it as follows:

"Disregard any movement of your hand. Do not think about it. It is important that you do not think but simply listen to my voice. Your part in this experiment is simply to listen to my voice and look ahead. All the time your left hand is growing heavier. Your right hand has an irresistible desire to move upward. You will feel the sensation in the muscles not only of your arm but your shoulder, and slowly the arm is starting to rise."

(In some subjects the movement will be imperceptible, and cannot be seen if you are looking at it directly from above, but can best be seen from the side. This should be watched very closely, as the fact should be allowed for that there may be an appreciable time lag between the suggestion being made and being acted upon.) Continue suggestions with: "There is a definite difference in the muscular tensions which are now controlling your arms. The muscles that are raising your arm are active without your wish, without your conscious control, and are now starting to raise your arm without any reference to what you feel, or what you think. You are merely an observer sitting quietly in the chair. Your breathing is deeper than usual and one arm is pressing heavily down on your left leg. It feels like a lump of lead, and your right arm feels as though it didn't belong to you, rising slowly, the whole of the time." This type of suggestion is continued until the arm moves, which it will in about three out of five people. If your subject's arm shows no sign of rising after about 15 minutes, tell him to rest—to close his eyes and forget all about his arms, and simply rest. Without disturbing him, tell him you were conducting a test—that it doesn't mean he is a good or bad subject—and to dismiss the matter from his mind and listen to your voice. Continue with trance deepening talk which is given later.

Method Nine [Diplomatic Approach to Difficult Subjects]

There are many individuals who have an unconscious resistance to being hypnotised, and with some of these people the following method will often succeed.

Some individuals may have a rebellion complex against authority or resent taking any form of orders from other people. Others may resist inductions because in dealing with nervous or emotional difficulties they may, by effort of will power over a long period, have built up a habit of self sufficiency or an attitude of independence.

Hypnotism can sometimes be successfully achieved with people of this nature by couching your suggestions in such a way as to challenge their self sufficiency or independence and pride. Appeals to pride can be made by telling this type of subject that the ability to be hypnotised depends on the intelligence possessed, and requires some power of concentration. The strategy is to challenge the subject's ideas of his ability to perform the tests and canalise his interest and endeavours. For instance, instead of telling him that his arm will get stiff and rigid, explain to him that if all intruding thoughts can be successfully inhibited, any suggestions made by the subject to himself become operative. Say to him: "Now I would like to see if you can make your arm rigid by the time I count ten. I want to see if you can concentrate sufficiently on the idea and make your arm so stiff that you will be unable to bend it." Once these contrary subjects have been successfully "misdirected," they can be influenced by the phrasing of suggestions in the above manner. Phrase all the suggestions in such a way as to make the subject feel that his power of concentration and ability to control his thoughts are being challenged.

Method Ten

Another method of inducing hypnosis featuring deep breathing, was widely used by some of the hypnotists in the last century. You can employ this method by following the instructions now given.

The subject is seated comfortably with legs stretched out, arms relaxed, head resting backward, and he is asked to take a deep breath, and addressed on lines similar to the following:

"That is right, now a deep breath this time—that is right, breathe in deeply—deeper—just hold it for a moment and then breathe out. I want you to listen to me and continue breathing in deeply as I say the words IN then OUT."

The suggestions are continued on the following lines: "Your arms and legs are getting heavy. The whole of your body is feeling heavier. Now close your eyes. Your head is feeling light and you may feel a little dizzy and detached." As the subject continues to breathe deeply the amount of oxygen in his blood stream is increased which produces a detached, hazy state of mind. The reader may prove this for himself by experimenting. Hypnotic suggestions are continued on the following lines. "Do not take notice of any noises. Just listen to my voice. Nothing is going to disturb you, you are just resting comfortably. Going further and further away into a deep, sound sleep."

CHAPTER SEVEN

SLEEP TO HYPNOSIS AND INSTANTANEOUS HYPNOSIS

It should be noted that to make any suggestions to a sleeping subject which would be resented by him if he were fully conscious, will bring into operation a resistance, and not only will the suggestions be ineffective, but the subject will in all probability wake up. This method would obviously not be used without the prior consent of the individual concerned, excepting of course under unusual circumstances, such as parents possessing some psychological knowledge and wishing to cure a child of some bad habit such as bed wetting.

Method of Operation

Do not begin to operate this method until the subject has been soundly asleep for at least an hour-and-a-half. If the subject is not used to you being in the room whilst he is asleep it is better if the induction is spaced over a period of a week or more. For the first approach, content yourself by merely entering the room and sitting for fifteen minutes or so at some distance from the bed in which the subject is sleeping. Do absolutely nothing. Content yourself for the first few sessions by carrying out the same procedure, but each time approaching nearer to where the subject is sleeping. If the approach you are making is slow and gradual, in a short time you should be able to sit on the bed of the sleeper without in any way disturbing him. When the subject is not roused from his sleep condition by your presence, you can finally address him in a quiet, low voice, or touch him without awakening him. The purpose of this slow approach is to accustom him to the slight sounds you will make by breathing, and moving, and so your presence does not disturb him. Under ordinary circumstances any unfamiliar sound or smell, such as a smell of fire, or a stranger entering the bedroom, would arouse the individual immediately. When the point is arrived at, in which the individual can be addressed in a quiet low voice, the required suggestions can be put that he is going to do as you suggest, .that he will be more confident, and is going to lose any bad habits. This method is especially suitable for a mother or nurse to use with children.

Method Twelve (Auditory Method)

There are a wide variety of methods which employ the sense of hearing. The basis of this method is monotony—this monotonous stimulation aided by suggestion often succeeds where other methods fail. The tick of a clock or a metronome, may be used. It is preferable that the tick should be slow. Suggestions may be employed at the same time so that the hypnotist's spoken suggestions and the ticks are both being heard simultaneously. Another method is to instruct the subject to imagine that the ticks are words, saying, for example, "You—are—going—to—sleep, you—are—going—to—sleep," so that they form a regular pattern.

Instantaneous Method

Sometimes a hypnotist may be seen to carry out a very rapid hypnotic induction. The induction may take place in one second, appearing to be instantaneous, and to the uninitiated seemingly bordering on magic.

Post Hypnotic Suggestion

These ultra rapid inductions may be brought about in two separate ways. In the first way the subject has been previously hypnotised, and a post hypnotic suggestion has been made to him that he will instantly pass into a hypnotic trance again at a given cue from the hypnotist. For example the hypnotist may, when the subject is hypnotised, tell him "In a few moments I am going to wake you, and afterwards if I say the word 'sleep' to you, you will immediately go into a hypnotic trance."

If the hypnotist after waking the subject, approaches him and says "sleep" the subject will immediately pass into a trance.

The hypnotic induction takes place instantaneously and is very spectacular, but in actual fact the same effect could be produced with the same subject simply by saying to him: "When I snap my fingers you will go fast asleep." If this were done, he would go into a trance just as rapidly. The whole secret of this is to choose a good hypnotic subject who has previously been hypnotised and who, in consequence of this, will pass again into a trance very quickly.

Spontaneous Somnambulists

In addition to the above method, a very rapid induction can be carried out on certain people who have never been previously hypnotised. These are a certain type of person who were described by Binet as Spontaneous Somnambulists. The triggering off of the trance is dependent on the skill and technique of the hypnotist.

Whilst in this Course I have advocated only conservative methods of hypnotic induction, I am, for record purposes giving the following description of this method of hypnotic induction, on the lines which it used to be performed by stage hypnotists, when they gave public demonstrations of hypnotism for entertainment. Quite rightly these demonstrations were banned by an Act of Parliament.

The hypnotist usually had his subject (perhaps victim would be a better word), close his eyes and stand stiffly to attention. Then, making a sudden noise, either by shouting or clapping his hands together, he swayed him rapidly backwards and laid him flat on the ground. The shock of the sudden noise, the closing of the eyes, the sudden movement backwards, plus the hypnotist's suggestions, all aided in disorientating the subject. From the point of view of a showman this type of induction was impressive but, it was not only a breach of good taste, but also a betrayal of the confidence placed in the hypnotist by the unsuspecting volunteer.

Drug Methods

A number of different drugs are used to produce changes in states of consciousness. Some of these states resemble hypnosis, but none are identical with hypnosis produced by the methods explained in this Course. The administration of most drugs necessitates medical knowledge and trance induction by these means does not come within the scope of this work.

Other Methods

It is reported that hypnosis can be produced by pressure on certain nerves, veins and arteries. There is no doubt that this is so, but it is doubtful whether the hypnotic state is attained as a direct result of these physical manipulations, or whether an intermediate submissive state is produced, from which the transition to the hypnotic trance is effected by forceful suggestion.

These physical means will be known to some physicians but in view of the attendant hazards of such methods, it is better they are disregarded, they are reported here simply to record them and to advise any students of the subject who may have heard of them not to be so ill advised as to attempt to experiment with them.

There are also some mechanical devices which are used as a means of inducing hypnosis. Among these are revolving discs, mirrors, artificial eyes and photographs of a hypnotist's eyes, but all of these visual methods have the very serious disadvantage of ceasing to be operative at the most vital and critical point in the induction which is, of course, when the subject closes his eyes.

There is no doubt that the soundest method of hypnotising a subject is a hypnotic induction. One of the author's hypnotic inductions on record and on tape recording is in regular use as a hypnotic conditioning method by many students of hypnosis and self hypnosis.

CHAPTER EIGHT

DEEPENING HYPNOTIC STATE

One of the most difficult tasks of the hypnotist is to determine the depth of hypnosis which he has produced in his subject. During the early stages of the induction, when the subject still has his eyes open, any dilation of the pupils or vacant look can be noted as disorientation takes place, but when the eyes are closed these clear and unmistakable signs are lacking.

Assessing Depth of Hypnotic State

The face in some people undergoes a distinct change as a somnambulistic and waxlike appearance is assumed. There are a number of reflex actions which take place such as fluttering of the eyelids, swallowing, twitching of the fingers and hands, and with some the face grows pale and the rate and depth of breathing often alters. There are frowns, blinks and other spasmodic movements which may be made by the subject, but to interpret what these denote is by no means an easy matter. Each individual under hypnosis reacts in an entirely different manner. The ability to judge the depth of trance is an ability which is developed by experience.

There are tests for gauging the depth of the hypnotic state, for example, telling your subject that his arm, without any volition on his part, will rise into the air, or, alternatively, that he is unable to get up from his chair or open his eyes. The degree in which your suggestions have been effective or partially effective can easily be seen, and are a clear indication of how deeply your subject is hypnotised.

Hypnotic Conditioning

It should be borne in mind that any successful test or experiment is, in itself, a form of hypnotic conditioning. For example, if the hypnotist holds the subject's arm rigidly sideways from his shoulder, and informs him that it will stay in this position, and the arm remains rigidly in this position, then, not only is it a test but also it pre-disposes the subject to accept the next suggestion.

When, by the breathing and general appearance of the subject, you judge that your suggestions have, in some measure been effective, you may proceed to carry out tests to ascertain and increase the depth of trance.

Rigid Arm Test

Take hold of the subject's arm and pull it out gently from the shoulder until it is fully extended. Give it a gentle shake whilst it is fully extended, as though implying by the movement that you wish it to remain stiffly extended. To amplify this point, if you raise the arm and suddenly let it go, it will, in all probability, drop, but if you raise the arm and support it for some seconds and firmly place it in an extended position, as though you expect it to stay there, then gently withdraw your hands, leaving it in that position, it will in all probability, remain so. There are subtle distinctions in the ways of handling, touching and moving people about, which can only be acquired by experience and shrewd observation. If, in response to this test, the subject's arm remains extended, you can firmly suggest to him that it is becoming fixed in this position and that, try as he may, he will be unable to put his arm down. Continue with these suggestions and, in all probability, he will be unable to do so. Let him try for five or ten seconds and then gently tell him that when you touch his arm it can be lowered. Take hold of his hand and, with your free hand, stroke his arm gently, lowering the rigid limb, at the same time saying: "The muscles in your arm are becoming limp and relaxed, and your arm will become perfectly normal and you can lower it quite easily."

Eye Closure Test

From this initial test you can then proceed to the suggestion of eye-closure. Say to your subject: "Your eyes are tightly closed. The lids are becoming tightly stuck together. In a few moments I am going to ask you to try to open them, but you will find that this is impossible. The harder you try, the more tightly closed they will become." Repeat these suggestions for a short time and then request the subject to try to open his eyes. When he has made an attempt for a short time, tell him to cease all effort and to relax and to go on resting. Follow this test up by the suggestion that he has become tightly stuck to the chair in which he is sitting, that his feet have become stuck to the floor, and he is unable to move the muscles in his legs, that the greater his efforts, the more tightly he will be held in the chair, as though he were pressed down by an invisible weight. Then ask him to try to stand. Continue your verbal suggestion, commenting on his inability to rise while he tries to do so. After he has tried and failed, tell him to relax and to listen to your voice. You may then inform him that he can speak without in any way disrupting his trance state. Ask him to start counting, but tell him that he will be unable to count beyond ten. In a large number of cases this will be so.

Conditioning By Hypnotic Sleep Walking

Return again to the test of being unable to get up from the chair. Repeat this test and when it has again been demonstrated to the subject that your suggestions have proved effective, instruct him to cease his efforts and relax. Then tell him that when you clap your hands together he will be able to stand up, and that you will take him by the arm and he will walk with you, and that he will grow sleepier with each step he takes. Then clap your hands and grasp him by the arm firmly and continue repeating your suggestions whilst you walk him for about a dozen paces or so and instruct him to stand still. Continue your suggestions that he will grow sleepier and sleepier. This conditioning deepens the trance.

As explained, the trance condition is deepened a little with each test. It must not, however, be assumed that the performance of a series of experiments will produce a hypnotised subject. Many subjects will act as though they were hypnotised and will carry out actions suggested to them, though, in actual fact, they are not deeply hypnotised. They will act a part because they feel it too much of an effort to resist the hypnotist's commands. It should be remembered that they wish to be hypnotised so that they may later gain the benefits of hypnotic suggestion. This compliance, if followed out, will lead to a deepening of the trance, but it should not be assumed that every subject who obeys commands is hypnotised. No two subjects ever act alike. The reader must use his own judgment in determining the depth of trance or, for that matter, whether his subject is hypnotised or not. This he can gauge from the reactions of the subject to his commands or to the tests. Generally speaking, there will be an appreciable pause before commands are carried out—often five or ten seconds' duration. The hypnotised subject has the appearance of heaviness and lethargy which would be hard to simulate. Once seen, the general characteristics are easily recognised and unmistakable. The reader, after a little experience, will choose and probably devise his own tests. By noting the reactions of various subjects on whom the tests are performed he will, in a very short time, be able to form an accurate opinion as to how deeply his subjects are effected by hypnosis.

Getting Subjects to Speak

If a subject is spoken to he will normally reply. If he does not do so, he may be told that he can speak and be asked to repeat a few words after the hypnotist, after which he can be asked questions. If any of the questions bear on matters which would render him uncomfortable, he will probably wake up. The voice of the hypnotised subject is characterised by a peculiar, dull flat tone, of a lower volume than his ordinary voice, sometimes it is almost inaudible. His general bearing is of lethargy, but this again cannot be taken as a guide for all subjects.

Caution on Demonstration

It is important when carrying out demonstrations to avoid causing a subject to perform any actions which are inimical to his dignity, or are, in any way, in bad taste. Non-observance of these points would not only break faith with your subject who has had sufficient confidence in you to place himself in your hands but will also alienate the more sensitive witnesses to your demonstration.

CHAPTER NINE

"INFORMAL" HYPNOSIS

The method of inducing a trance and deepening it simply by talking has many advantages. It has been called the "informal method," whilst the more active methods of test and experiments were given the name of "formal" hypnosis. This so-called informal hypnosis has many advantages in general medical practice. The prestige of the practitioner is likely to suffer reverses in practicing hypnotism where he fails to hypnotise a subject. The *British Medical Journal* as long ago as 19th August, 1949, in advocating the wider use of hypnotism among doctors wrote: "The technique of inducing the hypnotic state consists in telling the subject with the greatest conviction and impressiveness something that is not strictly true—for instance, that his limbs are feeling heavy, his lids drop, and he is becoming sleepy. Such things are said, and have to be said, in the hope that their saying will make them come true. Certain temperaments will find actions of this kind either antipathetic or ridiculous, and the technique cannot then be carried through with the inner certainty and self-assurance which are imperative for success." A skilful technique can avoid this apparent obstacle. By the use of purely verbal inductions a hypnotic subject need not be given the opportunity of seeing whether he can disobey the hypnotist's commands or instructions, and, in consequence of this, his views of how far he has, or has not, been affected hypnotically are likely to be unclear. Therapeutic suggestion can be very effectively administered while the subject is in this light or "informal" state of hypnosis. In many cases all that is necessary for successful treatment is the achievement of this light state of hypnosis.

Alteration in "Time Sense" of Subject

When you are speaking with the object of increasing the depth of trance, let your voice grow lower and lower until the volume is a little less than a whisper. Make frequent pauses. Let there be plenty of time for your subject to react to your suggestions. If you proceed too rapidly you will fail. Time must be given for a suggestion to register. Remember that usually the deeper the hypnotic state the longer will it take for your subject to respond. It is one of the characteristics of the hypnotic state that time values alter. If your suggestions follow each other rapidly, before the subject has had time to act on, or register one suggestion, you will be speaking to him of the next. You will, in effect, be cancelling out your own suggestions. There is another reason why plenty of time should be allowed for your suggestions to sink in. This is because the hypnotic subject will easily become confused if two ideas are introduced at the same time. He can only keep his attention on one idea, and is likely to become uneasy, disturbed or break the trance if you introduce too many ideas. Another reason for speaking slowly is that by inducing drowsiness and sleepiness you wish the subject's mind to work slowly. To achieve this effect you must speak slowly, quietly, and in a low voice, otherwise you are likely to keep his mind brisk and alert.

Deepening Hypnotic State

The light hypnotic state may be not very far removed from the ordinary waking state, but can be deepened merely by talking. These are the lines on which the talk should be based:

"You are sitting comfortably in your chair doing nothing but resting. You will hear my voice speaking to you all the time, but it will not disturb you. You will find as you sit there, that your mind is becoming sleepier. You will not try to think about what I am saying to you, but you will hear everything. As I talk you will find the heavy feeling in your arms and legs increases. With each breath you take you are slowly sinking down, sleepier and sleepier—One part of your mind is already asleep, but you will continue to hear everything I say. Your mental condition is one of quiet rest. You will shortly notice a numbness in your hands and feet. This numbness will start to creep up your arms and legs, until all your body feels numb, but it will not disturb you or make you uneasy. All you will want to do is to go on sinking down, getting sleepier and sleepier. Don't argue or reason with yourself or worry about anything. You are resting quietly, peacefully, and nothing will disturb you. The reason that we are doing this is that the suggestions I will make to you will help you. You will find this feeling of rest, of being drowsy, of being asleep and awake at the same time becomes more pleasant as time goes on. It is just as though you were sinking down quietly and peacefully into a deep, deep sleep, where nothing will worry you, nothing will disturb you—and all you will want to do is to go on resting and getting sleepier and sleepier. As you get sleepier, you will find that your breathing becomes deeper. Take no notice of this but continue to rest. Any noises which occur will seem a long way off and will not interest you at all. You will not be interested in anything except rest. You are getting sleepier and sleepier. You will notice that your body is relaxed and there is no tension present now in your body, your arms or your legs. You are beginning to learn how to "let go" completely, to sink down into a deep, deep sleep. Soon you will begin to feel very comfortable, warm, just as though you were sitting comfortably in front of a fire and feeling too tired to bother about anything except sinking down and going further and further away into a deep, sound sleep."

"You may feel a little dizzy or dreamy whilst I am talking, or my voice may seem to fade away at times, but you will take no notice of this for steadily and quietly you are sinking down sleepier and sleepier."

The reader is advised to write out and memorise some trance deepening material of the above nature, so that he may be ready to fluently make suggestions calculated to deepen the trance states he produces in his subjects.

CHAPTER TEN

HYPNOTIC DEMONSTRATIONS

There are two ways in which a hypnotic trance may be deepened. One is by "talking sleep," to the subject and the other is by having him perform a number of conditioning actions. Generally speaking the best technique should be built up from a combination of both these methods.

Some years ago excellent examples of hypnotic conditioning could be seen at public performances of hypnotic demonstrations at music halls by professional hypnotists.

Hypnotism Act 1952

These public performances of hypnotism for purposes of entertainment were prohibited by the Hypnotism Act of 1952. A copy of this Act is obtainable from Her Majesty's Stationery Office.

Stage Hypnotism

Various procedures were followed by the stage hypnotists; for example volunteers would be invited to come on to the stage to act as subjects. When the hypnotist had a sufficient number of volunteers he would begin the process of finding the best subjects. He would probably begin with some tests such as having the group as a whole clasp their hands together, and then, with great emphasis, inform them that their hands had become locked together and could not be unclasped. A few of the group would find that they could not unclasp their hands and would be noted as prospective subjects.

This was followed by a routine of relaxation or a series of tests on the lines of those already explained in earlier Sections. Those who responded well to the hypnotic suggestions were then given more attention, and the others disregarded or dismissed.

The stage hypnotist having, by means of these tests, located a group of the most susceptible of his volunteers, proceeded to have them carry out a further series of actions which deepened the hypnotic state. The antics which the volunteers were made to perform included being rooted to the floor—playing imaginary instruments — conducting imaginary orchestras — being attacked by swarms of bees—being intoxicated by drinking water—imagining they were babies and crying for their mothers—being rendered cataleptic and being sat upon or stood upon by the hypnotist, together with whatever actions the fertile imagination of the entertainer could devise to amuse his audience. Though some of these performances were vulgar and in the worst possible taste, they nevertheless presented an excellent opportunity of seeing the various stages or depths of the hypnotic state.

Indications of Depth of Hypnotic State

The following list sets out the reactions of the subject and is a general guide for indicating the progression of the depth of trance attained, but the reactions of individuals vary widely.

1 Disregard of surroundings and full attention on hypnotist.
2 Physical ease and relaxation.
3 Involuntary blinking of eyelids.
4 Swallowing reflex.
5 Closing of eyes (of own accord or by suggestion).
6 Complete physical relaxation.

  7　Involuntary deep breathing.

  8　Inability to open eyes, inability to unclasp hands when asked to try.

  9　Inability to move limbs or get up from chair when asked to try.

10　Loss of memory in trance.

11　A paralysis of vocal chords (induced by suggestion).

12　Analgesia in trance induced by suggestion (insensibility to pain).

13　On awakening simple post-hypnotic suggestions will be carried out.

14　Trunk catalepsy can be produced.

15　Auditory hallucinations in trance.

16　Post-hypnotic amnesia (loss of memory of incidents in trance).

17　Ridiculous post-hypnotic suggestions will be carried out.

18　Post-hypnotic analgesia.

19　Can open eyes and not break trance.

20　Visual hallucinations in trance.

21　Post-hypnotic auditory hallucinations.

22　Post-hypnotic visual hallucinations.

23　Complete somnambulism.

The professional entertainer had many advantages over the lay hypnotist or hypnotherapist, for any hypnotist who has the opportunity of selecting (or rejecting) his prospective hypnotic subjects from a crowd can, by eliminatory tests, choose only those who are most responsive to his suggestions. In consequence of this he is more certain to be able to hypnotise his subjects. He naturally does not go looking for difficult subjects but begins to work on the most tractable and responsive, for success with his first subject is important and influences the others.

Many factors operated in favour of the entertainer hypnotist. The emotional expectancy and the anticipatory excitement of the audience did much to arouse their latent superstition which was helpful in creating the trance state in many of the subjects. In addition to this was the fact that the hynotist was a showman with all the polished patter of the professional.

Public Interest in Hypnosis

The public interest in hypnotism is comparatively recent, dating from approximately 1946-47, and from then until the Hypnotism Act in 1952 when hypnotic entertainments ended, many thousands of people throughout Britain must have witnessed hypnotic demonstrations. Though these demonstrations offended many of the sensitive who felt it an affront to human dignity to see adults running around on their hands and knees, growling like tigers or passionately hugging broomsticks, there were some positive gains resulting from these demonstrations. Witnessing them convinced many people that hypnosis was a fact which had been much doubted before these public demonstrations. It is significant that since that date hypnosis is slowly but surely being used as a form of medical treatment.

CHAPTER ELEVEN

TERMINATING HYPNOTIC SESSION

Normally there will be no difficulty in waking a subject. The difficulty is to induce the trance, not to terminate it. To awaken the majority of subjects, the mere suggestion that they will open their eyes and be wide awake at a given cue (such as counting six, the word "six" serving as the cue) is all that is necessary to terminate the trance. This method will be successful with practically all subjects.

Arousing Subjects From Hypnotic State

It is a sound method, when instructing a subject, to tell him that you will count, but this time that you will count backwards, that you will count ten . . . nine . . . eight . . . and so on, and that when you arrive at the number "One" he will be wide awake, and that he will feel much better for having rested. Do not waken subjects too abruptly. It is better to err on the side of doing so too slowly, rather than too rapidly.

Arousing Deeply Hypnotised Subjects

If you are unable to wake a hypnotised subject, which is very unlikely, do not in any way be disturbed. See that he is resting comfortably and that he has no tight clothing, such as a necktie, to restrict his breathing. Then instruct him on these lines: "I am going to leave you to rest. In a short time you will find that you will become restless. You will not know why, but you will want to wake up. When you feel this restlessness you will start to count slowly to yourself, and you will find that when you get to nine and ten you will find yourself waking up. You will find that your eyelids begin to move as though they were going to open. By the time you get to fifteen "your eyes will open by themselves, and you will be wide awake." Then leave your subject and in all probability he will awaken after a short rest. If he does not do so, do not be at all disturbed but make arrangements so that he may be made comfortable either on a bed or a couch and give him the following instructions: "You will continue to rest and will shortly pass into a sound sleep, from which you will awaken, and feel refreshed." Do not let other people try to arouse him. The sleeper will awaken after a few minutes, or at most a few hours' sleep, and will do so whether the hypnotist is present or not.

No uneasiness should be entertained if a subject does not wake up immediately in response to your suggestions, for the trance state will of its own accord turn into ordinary sleep, from which your subject will wake in a perfectly normal manner. The length of time he will sleep will be dependent on how tired his body is. In this way hypnosis makes possible a degree of relaxation and recuperation which would not have been possible through his ordinary sleep.

Upon awakening from a hypnotic trance the subject undergoes a change in consciousness. This can be described as a regaining of will, of memory and of reasoning powers—a re-orientation or picking up of the threads of consciousness again. The time taken to awaken varies with different individuals.

After The Hypnotic Session

If any suggestions have been made to the hypnotised individual, the nature of which are antagonistic or contrary to his views, desires or interests, there is every probability of his harbouring a hostile feeling towards the hypnotist. He may be quite unconscious of this hostility, which may express itself in a variety of ways. He may, for example, be critical of the hypnotist or of his methods of procedure, and in consequence develop a mild resistance to the hypnotist's instructions to "wake up." If this occurs no uneasiness should be felt and the instructions given above should be followed.

Some people on awakening may express disappointment with the experience. They may insist that they had heard everything that went on, or that they were unaffected by the hypnotist. This arises out of misconceptions they entertain concerning the nature of hypnotism. The lack of consciousness and amnesia which they possibly anticipated is not experienced by some subjects until some hours have been spent in conditioning them. Nevertheless, though the individual may consciously believe that his trance was extremely light, or that he has not been hypnotically affected, the suggestions which have been made to him in most cases will exercise influence, that is unless the subject deliberately sets out very determinedly to prove that the suggestions will not work.

It will sometimes be the experience of the hypnotist that someone whom he has hypnotised will, on waking, insist that he has not been hypnotised. This attitude may be maintained even though it may be demonstrated to the subject that he cannot open his eyes. Even then some subjects will still insist that despite this evidence they could have opened their eyes, or stood up if they had wished. In these cases the character structure of the individual is such that he cannot admit that he has been dominated and was under the control of anyone else.

The majority of people who insist that they have only

experienced a light trance, should have the nature of the hypnotic trance explained to them, and should be told that it is perfectly normal that they should hear external noises and maintain rapport with the hypnotist.

Don't attempt to convince those who dogmatically maintain that they have not been hypnotised. Explanations will serve no useful purpose.

The popular idea of the hypnotised person remembering nothing on waking applies only to a few subjects. People's reactions differ. The majority remember most of what occurred when they are hypnotised, but in the main their recollections tend to be faulty. The fact must not be overlooked that our recollections in the waking state are likewise faulty. If, for example, a person is dozing, often he will indignantly deny the fact.

Some subjects, on awakening, can apparently remember everything that has occurred, but then the memories may fade in the manner a dream vanishes. Others on awakening may have no recollection, or a very hazy one, of what has occurred, but gradually detail comes back to them until they can recall everything that has happened.

Post-Hypnotic Suggestions of Amnesia

Suggestions made to the subject that he will forget everything that has occurred during the trance, may or may not be effective. The effectiveness of the inhibiting suggestion is determined by how it affects the subject's pride, sense of independence, interest, morals, conscience and general character structure, also the nature of the material to be repressed.

An amnesia whilst awake may be created in respect of the events occurring in a hypnotic trance, but in subsequent trances the events may be remembered.

In waking consciousness, after being hypnotised, the individual may often recall phrases or happenings which have occurred during the hypnotic trance, but he may attribute these phrases and incidents to the work of his own imagination, and be unaware that they are memory fragments of the trance. On the other hand, an hysterical subject is very likely to imagine during the hypnotic trance that incidents occurred which are purely products of his own imagination.

The Two Most Essential Rules in Hypnosis

On awakening a subject from the hypnotic state, the first question the hypnotist should ask himself is this: "Is the subject wide awake and thoroughly aroused from the hypnotic state?" He should reassure himself on this point and should, as an invariable rule, make certain that the subject is thoroughly wide awake, and that no trace of the hypnotic state remains, and also that there are no uncancelled post-hypnotic suggestions other than those designed for the subject's own good, such as being able to relax, etc.

Post-hypnotic suggestions are dealt with in the next chapter.

CHAPTER TWELVE

POST-HYPNOTIC SUGGESTIONS

Post-hypnotic suggestions are, in effect, "delayed-action" suggestions. They are the operating of hypnotic suggestions at a later date. For example, whilst a subject is hypnotised, suggestions may be made that when he is awakened he will perform some action at a given cue. The appointed time arrives and the subject, in a waking state and apparently fully possessed of his faculties, will carry out the appointed task. The suggestions need not be directed to the performance of a specific task, but to an attitude of mind. It may, for example, be suggested that the individual's attitude towards some fear will undergo a modification or change, and this—if there is no stronger counter-influence—will be so. Post-hypnotic suggestions, however, grow weaker with the passing of time. Therefore, they should be aimed at creating habits which enable the subject to adapt himself more satisfactorily to life. In this case they have every chance of being adopted in place of the previous faulty behaviour patterns. It is apparent that the mere repetition of general phrases such as: "You are feeling better," etc., have not the same value as suggestions which have been patiently and carefully prepared. Often to prepare these suggestions considerable time must be spent investigating the subject's symptoms and complaints, history, medical record, present environment with immediate obstacles and limitations, together with his whole attitude towards life.

Hypnotic Suggestions To Avoid

The suggestions which are made to a patient (for such he is if he is asking for assistance) must not only be things which he desires, but also those things which are capable of practical fulfilment—otherwise his condition will in no way be improved. It might be added in the framing of post-hypnotic suggestions definite instructions should be avoided which would directly alter the patient's life; that is to say, he should never be instructed to make a choice or a decision, i.e. change his employment, to marry, or to break off an association. A hypnotherapist who is consulted for aid is a technician being asked to make an adjustment in the mental and emotional life of the patient, so that the patient himself shall be able to live his own life confidently and with full volition and control, and to make his own decisions.

When a patient is being given palliative suggestions to allay anxiety, post-hypnotic suggestions are made in the following manner:

"In a few minutes I am going to wake you up, and when you awake you will find that a change has occurred. You will feel relieved and all traces of anxiety will have left you, and you will feel completely relaxed." This should be amplified at length on the lines of lessened tension and of physical and mental relaxation. The self-esteem and well-being of the subject must continually be kept in mind, and his confidence in, and assurance of the sympathetic attitude of the hypnotist must be maintained, otherwise suggestions made to him will have little real value. It is difficult to lay down hard and fast rules for administering hypnotic suggestions, as there are so many variable factors—the chief of which is the unconscious attitude of the patient.

Experimental Post-Hypnotic Suggestions

If, for experimental purposes, the hypnotist at any time tries out any experiments, he should see that there is no possibility of the subject "acting out" the "post-hypnotic suggestion" at a later date when he accidentally encounters the same cue. As for example, if the subject were told that when he saw a glass of water he would feel very hot, and the hypnotist forgets to remove this suggestion at the conclusion of the session, the subject might, some days later, be disturbed by a recurrence of the symptoms of increased temperature, induced by the sight of a glass of water. The hypnotist, therefore, having made any post-hypnotic suggestions, should as routine, take pains to cancel out all suggestions which are not designed for the well being of the subject.

It is wise to inform the subject later of the nature of suggestions which have been made to him whilst hypnotised. He may or may not remember them; if a deep state has been induced there may be amnesia, but this state is subject to change and he may later recall the suggestions. If, in these circumstances, he has not been fully informed by the hypnotist, the latter is likely to lose the subject's confidence.

Gaining Full Confidence of Subject

The object of the hypnotist is to gain the full and complete confidence of his subject. The suggestions made in the hypnotic state should be explained to the subject when he is awake, so that intellectually he is fully aware of the procedure of treatment. Consciously and subconsciously his motives are directed to, and should be working together for the same ends.

If post-hypnotic suggestions are made which would

create resistance on the part of the individual, he will become uneasy and make efforts to combat the impulse to perform any unwelcome suggestion. This tension and anxiety is, however, immediately resolved if the post-hypnotic suggestion is carried out. If the subject who has carried out a post-hypnotic suggestion is questioned as to why he has carried out the particular act, he will usually rationalise his actions and find the most ingenious explanations and excuses.

Persistence of Post-Hypnotic Suggestion

The effective duration of the post-hypnotic suggestion is to a very large extent determined by how it fits in with the character structure, tendencies and habits, of the individual, or how far it is in his interests. If post-hypnotic suggestions are in any way damaging or derogatory to his sense of self-esteem, they will tend to fade more rapidly than suggestions which would give pleasure or be profitable.

Post-hypnotic suggestions may, or may not, be recognised as such by the subject. He may, for example, (impelled by a post-hypnotic suggestion) have no idea why he has to rise and alter the hands of a clock, or to re-arrange the furniture. On the other hand, he may have a dim idea that he should do this, or even that it has been suggested to him during the hypnotic trance. In other words, post-hypnotic suggestions, like other hypnotic phenomena, produce varying reactions with different individuals.

CHAPTER THIRTEEN

SELF HYPNOSIS

One branch of hypnosis which has not received the attention it deserves is that of self hypnosis. As a result of using hypnosis in treating patients for over twenty years, it is my firm conviction that when instruction and coaching in self hypnosis is included as part of the hypnotic treatment, better and more permanent results are obtained.

There are, of course, exceptions when patients cannot be trusted to devise suggestions best suited to their needs and, in the case of these individuals, it is inadvisable to instruct them in these techniques.

Objects of Self Hypnosis

The main objective people have in mind when seeking hypnotic treatment is to cure some ailment, increase confidence or overcome some disability, in short, to gain more control over themselves . . . and certainly not to become robots, bereft of will power. As a result, for many people the idea of acquiring the ability to help oneself through self hypnosis has a strong appeal.

Whilst it is true that the hypnotherapist has sometimes to play the part of a "mental healer" when he cannot get his patient to co-operate by using self suggestion, he should, in my view, make every effort to explain the techniques of suggestion to his patient, and get him to carry out a daily session of self suggestion, for, in this way, the twin drawbacks of relapse and dependency on the hypnotist can be avoided. When the patient's aid is enlisted in this way his morale is strengthened by the fact that he is playing an active part in his own treatment, and he is also able to administer self suggestions on intimate or personal matters.

All Hypnosis is Self Hypnosis

It has been said that all hypnosis is basically self hypnosis, and there is much to support this view. It is the subject's belief and conviction that the hypnotist possesses the mysterious power to hypnotise people which in great measure invests him with this power. If the subject doubted the hypnotist's ability it is very unlikely he would be hypnotised.

Instruction and coaching patients in self hypnosis is greatly aided by the fact that when a trance has been attained, this "mysterious power" can be passed over to the patient by using post-hypnotic suggestions such as "You can do this yourself." As this opens up the very valuable auxiliary of self treatment, self hypnosis in my opinion is one of the most important branches of hypnosis.

Self Hypnosis in Africa and India

My belief in the value of self hypnosis was aroused many years ago as a result of my experiences when conducting hypnotic demonstrations during lecture tours, and in later years by witnessing the powerful effects produced by self suggestion when the impressionable imaginations and superstitions of various natives were influenced and manipulated by witch doctors and other indigenous medicine men and healers.

My belief in the power of self suggestion was further strengthened and confirmed by my own experience and training in Yoga in India, and again by the results achieved by members of classes whom I had instructed in the use of the techniques of self suggestion and self hypnosis, and lastly, by seeing daily the negative results of self suggestion in a wide variety of psychosomatic ailments and nervous troubles.

Example of Unconscious Self Hypnosis

One of the first examples of the power of self hynosis which I witnessed was in Sydney, Australia, many years ago. I was including a brief hypnotic demonstration in a lecture I was giving on psychology, and had called for some volunteers. Turning to one of the volunteers I made a motion of my hand for him to sit down. To my surprise he immediately went into a hypnotic trance. I had not spoken to him or tried in any way to hypnotise him. It was his own emotional expectation and mis-interpretation of my gesture which had caused him, unknowingly, to hypnotise himself. This volunteer was of the type in which the trance can be created immediately as described in earlier pages as the Instantaneous Method. The French psychologist, Janet, describes this type of hypnotic induction as instantaneous somnambulism, and it is an impressive example of self suggestion.

Again and again as I travelled in Australia, New Zealand, Africa and India, I found more and more corroboration of the power of self suggestion, not only in the results achieved and the changes made in their lives by members of the classes to whom I taught self hypnosis, but also in the lives of the followers of various religions and beliefs.

In Africa and India I took every opportunity of seeing indigenous healers, sadhus, witch doctors and medicine men, and all ceremonies concerned with healing sick people, and what I saw convinced me that suggestion and above all, self suggestion, was the all important factor in helping and healing those who sought their aid. Typical examples of self induced trances can be seen in the Indian religious ceremony of Kavady when the devotee renders his body insensitive to the pins which pierce his tongue and flesh. Somewhat similar ceremonies are to be seen amongst the Malays in the Khalifa where swords and fire are used during the ceremony. The African rituals are mainly concerned with dancing, drumming and chanting but in all these the repetitive drumming, dancing and chanting produce trances in many of those taking part.

Common Denominator Is Self Induced Trance

However dissimilar the above ceremonies might appear they have much in common, for most of the people taking part in them are seeking a cure for some sickness and the indigenous practitioner, whether he is a priest, medicine man or witch doctor, conducts a ceremony or ritual which is linked up with the tribal, religious or cultural beliefs and superstitions of the devotee or supplicant. These are the beliefs in which the follower or "patient" has been brought up, and he will conform and follow the ritual of dancing, chanting or whatever it may be, and after a while goes into a trance state (that is to say he has, in a greater or lesser degree, been hypnotised) and if he is a good subject and his complaint is psychosomatic, there is every probability of what in medical terminology is described as a spontaneous cure.

However bizarre the methods of these empiric practitioners might appear to Western eyes, they achieve about the same percentage of results as Western therapists, for psychosomatic ailments afflict the superstitious and the sophisticated alike.

Difference Is In Name Not Nature of Hypnotic State

Allowing for the more flamboyant procedures and colourful rituals, also for greater superstition and undeveloped critical faculty on the part of simpler people, the distinction between the creation of the trance state through native rituals and through clinical hypnosis is more a matter of terminology than any real or intrinsic difference.

From my own experiences in Yoga I came to the conclusion that the lower stages of the yogic trance are identical with what we in the West term self hypnosis. I think it is essential to keep in mind that no one school of psychology or any religious belief or philosophy, has a monopoly of the trance state which is a universal mental phenomenon observable in people of all races and of all levels of intelligence.

The trance, or self induced hypnotic state, can be achieved in a variety of ways, varying from religious ritual to a clinical hypnotic induction. It is also attributed to many different causes. Some people believe it is caused by the Gods, others by magic or spirits or just by self suggestion. It should be borne in mind that when attained, the trance state can be used to produce very different objectives, for instance insensibility to pain (analgesia), singlemindedness in study, a cure for some ailment, increased confidence, conducting research into Extra Sensory Perception or, as in Yoga, to develop spiritually.

The student hypnotist will find many advantages in learning all he can about self hypnosis, for in doing so he has the opportunity of playing the dual role of hypnotist and subject and also is able to make use of the techniques of self hypnosis and self suggestion in his own life.

CHAPTER FOURTEEN

INSTRUCTION IN SELF HYPNOSIS

The easiest way to help a good hypnotic subject to learn self hypnosis is to include in the induction a post-hypnotic suggestion such as "You will be able to hypnotise yourself." This is, of course, not all that is required, for it is also necessary to give some explanation and instruction on the lines which follow. It sounds very easy to give a simple post-hypnotic suggestion on the above lines, and then prescribe a simple ritual such as counting and including a phrase such as "and when you get to ten you will drift off into a hypnotic state and be able to make your own hypnotic suggestions to yourself," but it is not quite as easy as this, for a number of important points must be taken into consideration.

Protective Post-hypnotic Suggestions

As I have mentioned previously unless you consider the hypnotic subject is capable and realistic, and not likely to make foolish suggestions which could be harmful, it is inadvisable to teach him self hypnosis. Again, in the interests of those who are taught self hypnosis, a number of self protective suggestions can be included such as "If anyone should knock on the door, or enter the room in which you are carrying out a self suggestion session, you will become instantly wide awake and alert." Also when giving these protective post hypnotic suggestions to your subject you can include "If at any time, whilst you are in a self induced hypnotic state, you overhear any remarks, they will not influence you."

This later links up with a further suggestion of "only thoughts which are constructive and for your own good, will register in your unconscious mind." Another protective suggestion which can be included to prevent advantage being taken of the increased suggestibility created in your patient is, "No one will be able to hypnotise you unless you specifically ask for this to be done." If you should feel that an absolute veto is indicated, make the post-hypnotic suggestion. "No one will be able to hypnotise you unless you make the request in writing. If it is necessary for dental work or any other reason, you will write your request and give it to your doctor or hypnotherapist."

Another suggestion which is advisable with some people is to include something on the following lines, "You will never have any difficulty in waking yourself . . . if you do go into a deep hypnotic state it will turn into a normal sleep from which you will wake refreshed and in a perfectly normal manner".

Instructing Student In Self Hypnosis

When beginning instructions on methods of self hypnosis, if your subject or patient has no general acquaintance with psychological ideas, I would recommend that you start by giving him a general idea of how the unconscious mind controls and influences many of our bodily functions, moods and mental attitudes, and then explain to him how, through using self suggestion, this unconscious mind itself can be influenced.

Difference Between Talking To And TELLING People

The manner in which a hypnotist or hypnotherapist talks to his patient alters. One moment he is explaining or describing something and offering reasons, reassurances or proof of the soundness and the truth of what he says, in short, submitting what he says to the patient's critical faculty, and the next moment he is speaking in an authoritative fashion, with no intention or desire that what he says should be analysed or argued about.

Broadly speaking we could say when talking to people that we either submit what we are saying to their critical minds, or completely disregard the individual's attitude and TELL HIM. Very often in hypnotic treatment it is helpful to use this more emphatic or authoritative way of talking. This does not mean raising one's voice or being unduly emphatic, otherwise resistances or resentment might be aroused. When we explain anything to people they participate by thinking about what we say but when we *tell them* they play a purely passive role of acceptance.

When instructing in self hypnosis it is better to err on the side of being authoritative rather than too friendly and informal. Avoid smiling or making long pauses, for the hypnotist who smiles or is uneasy or hesitant makes his own work more difficult. The objective is, without arousing any resistance or resentment, to convey in your manner a firm authoritative attitude, and whilst being reassuring, not being too informal.

This more authoritative style of talking is determined not only by the tone of the voice but also by the choice of words, and in the following advice about instructing a patient in the hypnotic techniques, I have enclosed much of the text in quotation marks, to indicate that the remarks are intended as an indication of the way in which to talk to a subject, and are not addressed to the reader.

Text For Instructing Student

After making some introductory remarks about the unconscious mind and explaining how it can be influenced by hypnotic suggestion, I recommend beginning on the following lines: "You can help yourself a great deal by using self hypnosis. After I have explained more about self hypnosis, I will hypnotise you and make post-hypnotic suggestions to you that you will be able to hypnotise yourself. This will enable you to give yourself a hypnotic treatment every day if you wish to do so. Once you have mastered these techniques you will not need my help."

Describing The Hypnotic State

"When I hypnotise you, or you hypnotise yourself, you must not have the expectation of going off into some extraordinary mystical realm. It is simply a pleasant, relaxed experience. Actually you pass through this state twice every day without being aware of it ... once when you wake up in the morning and again when you go to sleep. This transition from sleep to waking is not as sudden as it appears. Just as we drop off to sleep there is a rapid fading out of awareness, but briefly, just before we lose consciousness, we pass through what is called a hypnogogic state of consciousness. This is the borderland between the conscious and the unconscious mind, but our passage through this state is so brief that on awakening we have no memory of it.

"In the hypnotic and self induced hypnotic states normal consciousness is withdrawn and sinks, as it were, beneath the surface of your mind until it approaches the borderland or no-man's-land which divides your conscious from your unconscious mind ... but, instead of sinking into oblivion, awareness remains poised midway between the conscious and the unconscious mind, and linked with both. It is because it is linked with both that it can relay instructions and suggestions to your unconscious mind.

"This relaying is carried out by letting your suggestions silently pass through your mind. In this state you are talking to yourself, and this is actually what is happening, for your conscious mind is talking to, or instructing your unconscious mind what to do. You could think of your conscious mind as the one who plans, like the manager of a business, and your unconscious mind as the workers. Sometimes the manager has to go down to the workshops himself and instruct the workers. In a similar way this is what you will be doing when you let yourself sink into a hypnotic state, and your awareness approaches the borderland of the unconscious mind and gives it orders.

Reassuring Your Subject

"Do not feel uneasy when I hypnotise you, or when you hypnotise yourself, for I will make suggestions which will safeguard you." If your subject shows any signs of being ill at ease, ask him if he has any misgivings or doubts. Say to him "Do not feel uneasy, no harm can come to you. When I hypnotise you I will make suggestions that you will relax and be at ease. Even without my suggestions part of your unconscious mind will remain alert like a sentinel, just as it does when you are asleep. If this awareness did not remain you would have no memory of dreaming, nor would you be awakened by any sudden noises. One part of your unconscious mind will be on duty to protect you whether you are hypnotised or asleep. You are asking your unconscious mind for its help and you must trust it to look after you. If you go into a deep trance when you hypnotise yourself it will turn into normal sleep."

Practical Arrangements

Make arrangements that the room in which you are conducting the hypnotic session is quiet, and that there is not likely to be any interruptions, also that the room is neither too hot nor too cold, and above all, that there are no draughts.

See that your subject is comfortably seated or lying down whilst you are making these introductory remarks. Tell him to relax whilst he is listening to you and, in this way, he will become more at ease, and more amenable to, and ready for your hypnotic induction.

No two hypnotists work alike for the simple reason that each one develops his own technique according to his personality and experience. An excellent way in which to commence an induction is to ask your subject to take a number of deep breaths. You can then begin to take control by saying "Now breathe in . . . deeper . . . deeper . . . that's right, now out . . . slowly . . . now in again." In this way, without any sudden take over, you can quietly assume an authoritative role and your induction will commence smoothly, easily and naturally.

Hypnotising Subject

Assuming that you are using a fixed gaze method of hypnotising, as instructed in an earlier chapter, hold some object—a ring or a pen will do—about eighteen inches in front of your subject's face, slightly above his eye level, so that he has to look slightly upwards. Then slowly move the object about six inches to the right, and then back to centre, then to the left. Move it slowly from side to side, telling your subject to keep his eyes fixed on it. Whilst you are doing this and his attention is focused on the object you are holding, continue talking and, in this fashion, you begin to create a split in his consciousness. Tell him that soon his eyes will begin to tire, and that involuntarily he will blink. When he does so tell him that his eyelids will begin to feel very heavy, and that it will become more and more of an effort for him to open his eyes. Keep on telling him this, varying your wording.

Soon his eyes will tire, partly because of the slight strain of the eyes being directed upwards, and partly because of the nearness of the object on which they are focused. You can, without the subject's knowledge, increase this strain whilst moving the object from side to side, by moving it slightly upwards and nearer to your subject's face. This increases the strain on the eye muscles.

The periods for which your subject's eyes will close will become longer. When this happens and you detect signs that his eyes are fatigued, tell him to rest with his eyes closed, and continue talking on the lines of the material given in earlier chapters for deepening the hypnotic state. To bring about this induction in which you are teaching self hypnosis you can use the above, or other methods of hypnotic induction described in Chapters Five and Six, but with practice you will soon begin to experiment with methods of your own.

Deepening Hypnotic State

Continue with your suggestions for deepening the hypnotic state until you judge from signs such as the head lolling over, or the body slumping or other obvious signs that your subject is hypnotised. If you are not sure continue with your suggestions, or you can make some tests, but it is best if you are uncertain whether your subject is hypnotised, to phrase your suggestions in such a way that he cannot disprove what you tell him. For example if you say "You cannot raise your arm" and he immediately raises his arm, which he may do if he is only lightly affected, your authority is weakened. If you are not certain it is more prudent to continue with the trance deepening suggestions for a longer period before making any positive tests. When you feel the subject is sufficiently relaxed begin to make the suggestions he has requested you to make, or make those which you judge would be helpful. When you have completed these, make the post-hypnotic suggestions that he will be able to induce this hypnotic state in himself and register suggestions in his own unconscious mind.

Post-hypnotic Suggestions For Self Hypnosis

It is better to give precise instructions on just how your subject is to carry out his self suggestion sessions. Prescribe a definite routine such as "When you are about to begin a self hypnotic session breathe deeply ten times, and as you do so you will begin to feel relaxed and sleepy. If you are lying down look at the ceiling, or if you are sitting, look straight ahead and count silently to yourself. When you get to 'ten' your eyes will close by themselves and you will then go on counting silently to yourself, getting sleepier and sleepier as you count. When you reach 'twenty' stop counting and rest, for you will have sunk down deeply enough to register suggestions in your unconscious mind."

Then remind him "When you reach this detached state, however light or deep it may be, this is when you let your suggestions float silently through your mind in the way I have already described to you."

Post-hypnotic Suggestions for Subject to Terminate a Self Hypnotic Session

Make post-hypnotic suggestions to your subject that he will never have any difficulty in waking himself from the hypnotic state. Prescribe some simple routine which he is to use to terminate his hypnotic sessions, such as counting backwards from "five" and that at "one" he will be alert and wide awake.

After you have concluded your hypnotic session with your subject and he is wide awake, check that he understands the routine of hypnotising himself, also of the way in which he is to rouse himself. It is also sound practice to have him go through the routine self induction in your presence, to make sure there are no points on which he is not clear. Impress on your subject that, even if he has been only lightly affected by hypnotic suggestions, the suggestions will "get through" to his unconscious mind. Even if subjects have been hypnotically affected only in a mild degree, the most surprising benefits from this self treatment very frequently come about.

Uses of Self Hypnosis

Self hypnosis has great value where a number of treatments are required, as in complaints of long standing, where time is necessary for the desired changes to come about, or in weight reducing or altering some habit, which might be as slow in going as it was in forming.

Self hypnosis is an invaluable method of treatment, for once the patient has been instructed and advised of the way in which he is to work, he can administer a hypnotic or a self suggestion session as often as desired, without the time and expense of visiting a hypno-therapist.

*Fully detailed techniques are described in *Self Hypnosis and Scientific Self Suggestion,* by W. J. Ousby.

CHAPTER FIFTEEN

HYPNOSIS AND HEALTH SERVICES

It is frequently stated by medical authorities, that a large proportion of illness today is caused by mental stress and emotional conflicts, and I have seen it estimated that approximately 60 per cent of our hospital beds are occupied by sufferers from this type of illness.

At the same time as illness of this type increases we are faced with the prospect of a critical shortage of doctors for some years to come. Implicit in the two above statements is the distressing fact that during the next few years an increasing number of sick people will, through lack of personnel, not receive the treatment they require. This unpleasant fact is, unfortunately, one of the many problems which must be faced in a rapidly developing society.

There is talk at the present time of a possible collapse of the National Health Service, but whether this happens or not, the unalterable fact remains that for some years to come there will be a shortage of doctors, and a steadily increasing number of sufferers from psychosomatic illness, and in considering this disturbing picture of the nation's health, it appears that a valuable means of aiding overworked doctors and of making therapy available to large numbers of people has not yet been fully recognised.

The views I am putting forward in this chapter are the results of over twenty years of therapeutic work. It is my experience that groups of people can be instructed in hypnotherapeutic techniques, and in this way learn to help themselves. If these methods were employed in the Health Services, particularly in the Preventive Health Service, they would bring about a short cut in psychotherapy comparable with some of the dramatic results achieved by antibiotics in the treatment of physical complaints.

The following proposals do not suggest that laymen should diagnose or give medical treatment, but that, working under the supervision of doctors, a register of approved hypnotherapists could give aid to many people who, because of lack of therapists, are unlikely to receive the psychological aid they require.

Hypnosis Is Not a "Cure All"

It is not for a moment suggested that hypnosis is a panacea for all illness, but, as many of today's ailments are caused by stress, worry and nervous tension, if those people who are likely at a later date to suffer illness on this account, could be instructed in relaxation and self suggestion techniques before their illness developed, much of today's psychosomatic ailments would be aborted or would never occur.

Prevention Is Better Than Cure

An expanded Preventive Health Service, incorporating group therapy using relaxation and self hypnotic and self suggestion techniques, could take much work off the shoulders of overworked doctors, who could send patients to groups where they could be instructed in relaxation techniques and coached in positive self suggestion.

Group Treatment in Self Hypnosis Could Provide a Short Cut

I know from personal experience that groups consisting of from ten to twenty people can be instructed in these techniques, and have conducted such groups in Australia, New Zealand, South Africa, Rhodesia, Kenya and Britain for a number of years. My experience is that most people dealing with stress, nervous tension and emotional problems require tuition in the personality skills of relaxation and self suggestion rather than treatment.

Despite all our scientific and technological advances, psychologically speaking, we are still in the "dark ages." We get an instruction book with a motor car or a sewing machine, but with ourselves, "the human machine," we get no such instructions.

Every human being will inevitably be faced with problems . . . problems of adolescence, of marriage, of parenthood, of middle age and of old age. If the individual is handicapped by some emotional trauma or other disability, these crises will exert greater strain. It is in the absence of such instruction that most psychosomatic illnesses develop, and yet they could be averted or absorbed by reassurance, relaxation instruction and tuition in self suggestion techniques.

In most cases a few hours instruction in relaxation, self suggestion or self hypnosis would prevent many people suffering years of misery, ill health and eventual breakdown, save doctors a great deal of time and the nation untold man hours.

Mass Hypnosis On Radio

Reverting to the practicality of such schemes, as far back as 1948 whilst on a lecture tour, I was invited by the New Zealand Government Radio Services to broadcast a programme to explain and coach listeners in some simple relaxation techniques, and also to carry out a mass hypnotic session over the radio, broadcasting suggestions of general relaxation and of general mental and physical welfare. This broadcast was well received as will be seen from the following letter from the New Zealand Broadcasting Services:

20th December, 1948

Dear Mr. Ousby,

As you were unable to check the results of your broadcast from Station 1 ZB before departing from New Zealand, I thought you would be interested to know how the listeners reacted.

The general tenor of coment in the mail received indicates that those who wrote enjoyed the relaxation brought about by your broadcast and thereby obtained beneficial results. As I indicated whilst you were here, I am sure that a series of treatments of this nature would bring about permanent relief to a lot of people.

We have not had one word of criticism or any unfavourable reaction of any kind to your programme, and I trust that when you return to New Zealand we will be able to broadcast a further series.

With best wishes,

Yours sincerely,

(signed) J. W. Griffiths
Station Manager, 1ZB

Auxiliary Medical Register of Hypnotherapists?

I am not for a moment suggesting that anyone but doctors should supervise this therapeutic work, but it would be to the benefit of all if a register of experienced hypnotherapists was formed and they were recruited into some Auxiliary Medical Register as a branch of the Preventive Health Service. I am sure that most hypnotherapists would, like myself, be willing to devote certain hours to such work on a voluntary basis in order to assist in the formation of such a scheme.

The advantages of hynotherapists being available at clinics where group therapy was being carried out would be that

(a) Doctors could send along tense and worried patients or those suffering from psychosomatic complaints to be taught how to relax and to be initiated in the self suggestion techniques so that they could help themselves by positive suggestions instead of unconsciously bringing about self induced illness.

(b) People who are at present unable to receive psychological aid because of shortage of therapists could receive reassurance through relaxation therapy pending psychiatric treatment.

(c) Further use could be made of such a register by hypnotherapists being attached to, or visiting hospitals to give hypnotic treatment to specified patients to prevent them from worrying and to help them to relax and to co-operate in treatment. Hypnotic suggestions would have very great value in reassuring those who have operations pending, and in helping in rehabilitation and in adjusting the mental attitudes of those who have to make terms with some permanent disability.

(d) Another very great service hypnosis could render would be to those who are fatally ill or about to die. Hypnotic suggestion could make their last hours easier. Their minds and bodies could be eased and courage and comfort given, particularly by therapists who themselves have strong beliefs in the meaning and purpose of life.

Hypnotherapy and the National Health Service

At the present time psychotherapy is the weak point in the nation's armoury in the fight against ill health ... for many illnesses are caused by mental and emotional stresses.

It is no dream to say that the hypnotherapeutic techniques (which in my view include relaxation, auto suggestion, self hypnosis and hetero hypnosis) could be a most powerful aid in strengthening this weak point in our medical services. This powerful aid is the healing force of Nature herself ... for just as broken bones will knit and torn flesh will heal, in the same way given the right conditions, nature will also soothe the nervous system, restore emotional equilibrium nad bring peace of mind.

Hypnosis is a natural healing agent which, correctly prescribed and administered, can, in a perfectly natural way, bring about a harmonious functioning of the mental, emotional and physical functions.

Sooner or later hypnosis will undoubtedly take its place in the National Health Service, and the sooner this happens the fewer will be the number of people who will suffer emotional distress and physical illness.

CHAPTER SIXTEEN

CONCLUSION

It is important that the student hypnotist should take his responsibilities seriously, and give very careful consideration to all the suggestions he will be making to his subjects.

The following are a number of points which should be kept in mind:

* Never attempt to hypnotise an unco-operative subject.
* Never hypnotise minors or children unless in the presence of parents or responsible witnesses.
* Obtain the permission or agreement of the husband, wife or parent of anyone who might be thought not to be a completely free agent.
* Get the subject's agreement, request or consent for the nature of the hypnotic suggestions which might affect his future life.
* At the end of each hypnotic session, see that your subject is fully awake and acting normally in every way before he leaves you.
* See that all the suggestions and post-hypnotic suggestions you have made to your subject during a session are cancelled, excepting, of course, those which are for his own good.
* Avoid use of the fixed-gaze methods with people whose eyes are weak, or who appear to be unusually nervous.
* Hypnotism is more easily induced in people who are expecting it to help them. There is an exception to this where the desire to receive help causes

over-eagerness or an anxious, nervous or tense condition.

* The first time an attempt is made to hypnotise a subject there may be a difficulty in inducing the trance. If the subject is not a good subject during the first induction, he may be only very lightly affected by your suggestions. On the second and third attempts the suggestions will have greater effect. Once any depth of trance has been effected, subsequent inductions become easier and easier. Post-hypnotic suggestions may be employed to deepen later trances, and facilitate the ease with which they may be induced. In the absence of any counter influences affecting the subject each successive trance becomes easier to induce.

* When you are carrying out experiments, tests, and attempting inductions, many unexpected incidents are likely to occur. If you are unprepared for them you may find yourself embarrassed or disconcerted. It is impossible to anticipate everything which is likely to happen. Therefore do not, in any way, be disconcerted. Preserve an appearance of perfect calm and self control, and maintain your prestige.

Policy and Suggestions on Giving Advice

A hypnotist may find that he is called upon to give advice upon a variety of subjects. These may cover illness, personal and domestic troubles, and occupational difficulties. So it is as well to have a set policy ready, and to observe it at all times. Make sure that anyone seeking advice on any matter affecting his health has seen his own doctor.

Do not give direct advice on major problems such as counselling a change of occupation or refusing an offer of other employment. In particular, avoid giving direct advice, or a decision, on domestic problems. Do not place yourself in a position whereby anyone later on may be enabled to say: "I did as you told me. Look what has happened. It's your fault!"

When you do express opinions, always give reasons for your views. It is wisest to explain all the factors of a case clearly, and to leave it to the subject to arrive at the right solution. Until the hypnotist is quite sure of the circumstances he is dealing with, he should avoid making specific suggestions.

Personal Beliefs

Care must be taken to ascertain the religious, social and political beliefs of a subject in order to avoid offending or making any suggestion incompatible with his beliefs, or injuring his susceptibilities.

Avoidance of Development of a Dependency

The hypnotist must avoid, at all costs, allowing the subject to unconsciously slip into the habit of considering the hypnotist indispensable to him. It is very easy, and often beneficial to the subject, to look upon the therapist as his guide, philosopher and friend, but it is undesirable that he should think that the hypnotist is indispensable to his daily living, and that he cannot get along without him. This, obviously, is inimical to the final objective, for the aim is to build up in the subject self-confidence and self-reliance. For this reason, the hypnotist must be on his guard against giving out too much help from the beginning of the contact, and this must be gradually decreased as progress is made.

Demonstration of Physical Feats of Strength

If subjected to excessive strain, bones can break and tissues can be injured whether a person is hypnotised or not. To avoid any possibility of injury do not attempt to cause a hypnotised subject to undertake unreasonable feats of strength. It is quite obvious that not only would such an occurrence be dangerous and distressing to the subject, but it would also be very damaging to the hypnotist. Carelessly or thoughtlessly planned experiments of this nature give much material for adverse criticism of hypnotism. In any experiments where some degree of muscular effort is required, enlist as your volunteers only strong young people.

Therapeutic Suggestions

If anyone should ask for hypnotic suggestions to remove pain, or to alleviate or cure an ailment, no hypnotist should ever do so without making further enquiries into the circumstances of the cause. Pain is usually nature's warning that something is wrong, and it would be wrong to block it out with hypnotic suggestions without enquiring further.

The hypnotist should, by asking the patient, discover how long the prospective subject has had his pain or symptoms, and what treatment he has received for it. From this information he will be in a better position to decide what he should do. For example, a headache might be nothing more than a temporary hangover from a late night, but, on the other hand, if it was recurrent or has been persistent it might possibly be the beginning of a brain tumour. A stomach-ache might be a temporary colic but, if the pain is severe, it could be an acute attack of appendicitis, and in the patient's own interest it would be better that he should see a doctor as soon as possible. If you decide to use hypnosis then suggestions should be made on the following lines, "Your pain will grow easier, but this will not make you cancel your intention to see your doctor. The relief from pain will last until you see your doctor but you must go and see him."

It is hardly necessary to point out that anyone intending to give therapeutic suggestions would be wise to become acquainted with the ground work of psychology and have a doctor whom, if necessary, could be approached for advice.

If a hypnotist is approached for help by some sufferer who has exhausted all possible orthodox methods of treatment without success, no objection can be taken to the hypnotist rendering what aid he can. He will find that in a number of cases he is able, if not to cure, to alleviate many complaints. If possible the hypnotist should attempt to get the unofficial blessing of the patient's own doctor.

* Hypnotism should not be regarded as a new means of living one's life or achieving objectives. It is a means to an end. The life of any individual should be lived, arranged and organised in full waking consciousness, and should be so constituted that he may live naturally and spontaneously. Hypnotism is only a means of building the habits necessary to live in a healthy, balanced manner. It is also a means of removing obstacles, habits and ideas which will interfere with this process.

* In learning to hypnotise people various difficulties and obstacles may arise to delay competence being achieved. Circumstances may interfere with the programme planned, opportunities for practice or suitable subjects may not be available. These set-

backs will adversely affect the beginner if he has not grasped the fact that he is also vulnerable to suggestion. If obstacles and delays occur—do not be discouraged. Once he encounters a good somnambulist, if he has followed the instructions with only moderate competence, he cannot fail to achieve a successful induction. Once this is accomplished his confidence will be established, and his failures forgotten. How soon he discovers his first somnambulist is simply a matter of luck—and perseverance.